CRITICAL THINKING ACTIVITIES

IN
PATTERNS,
IMAGERY,
LOGIC

Dale Seymour

Ed Beardslee

DALE SEYMOUR PUBLICATIONS

Approximately half the activities in this book were originally designed by the Dale Seymour Publications staff as ancillary materials for Silver Burdett Mathematics, copyright 1987 by Silver Burdett and Ginn. Development was done with the understanding that the two companies share joint ownership of the activities, and that each company has the right to publish the activities in its own format. Dale Seymour Publications gratefully acknowledges the support of Silver Burdett and Ginn in the development and production of the initial phase of this project. The following pages are copyright 1987 by Silver Burdett and Ginn: 2, 5, 7, 8, 9, 10, 12, 14, 16, 17, 18, 19, 20, 22, 26, 28, 30, 32, 33, 35, 37, 39, 41, 43, 54, 56, 57, 58, 62, 65, 67, 69, 73, 75, 78, 79, 80, 82, 83, 84, 85, 89, 90, 92, 101, 102, 104, 105, 107, 109, 111, 114, 116, 117, 119, 121, 122, 123, 125, 127, 129, 132, 134, 136, 137, 139, 140, 141, 143, 145, 147, 148, 151, 153, 154, 156.

Cover design by Rachel Gage

DS01815
ISBN 0-86651-440-6

DALE
SEYMOUR
PUBLICATIONS
P.O. BOX 10888
PALO ALTO, CA 94303

10 11 12 13 14 15-MA-95

CONTENTS

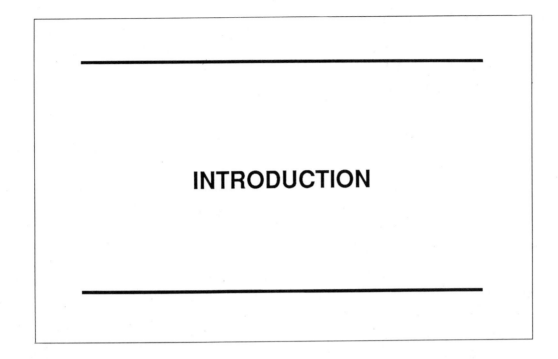

INTRODUCTION

Thinking skills and problem solving are currently given high priority in curriculum development and inservice programs. Although each area of the curriculum defines and approaches thinking skills and problem solving somewhat differently, the basic emphasis on teaching students how to think and how to learn has strong support from most people concerned with the education of youngsters.

Too often, thinking skills have been overlooked or considered extra, something above and beyond the basics that must be taught. Teachers need to recognize that thinking skills *are* basic. The term *critical thinking skills* is a good one because the word *critical* has a number of different meanings. It means *analytical,* and it means *evaluative* or *judgmental,* but it also means *indispensable, vital, essential.* Indeed critical thinking activities should be considered indispensable to the education of every child.

This book presents activities to help students develop their thinking and problem-solving skills. Mathematics curriculum specialists have identified from ten to fifteen strategies that can help students solve nonroutine math problems. Often students may need to use more than one such strategy to arrive at the solution for a given problem. Some of these strategies require that students use skills such as thinking visually, recognizing patterns, using logical reasoning, and doing organized counting—all of which are elements of critical thinking in mathematics.

There are a number of different ways to categorize thinking skills. No two authors would choose the same list or prioritize the importance of each skill in the same way. This book concentrates on three specific types of thinking skills: *patterns, imagery,* and *logic.* If students are to become successful problem solvers, they need to become good critical thinkers at the same time.

How to Use This Book

As a supplement to a regular textbook this book provides materials that can be used in a variety of ways to introduce, reinforce, and elaborate on specific critical thinking skills.

Reproducible Pages

The pages in this book are designed to be photocopied for distribution to students as individual worksheets or problem cards. Preparing a transparency of any page (using a photocopy machine and transparency acetate) makes it possible to present a lesson to a group or to the entire class by using a overhead projector.

Sequence

In general, there is no recommended sequence for presenting the topics or the activities within a single topic. Teachers may choose and order the activities in whatever way they believe will best meet their instructional goals. Activities within a topic are generally ordered from simpler to more difficult, as indicated by their one-star, two-star, or three-star rating.

Class Discussion

Students develop their thinking skills by observing how other people think. For this reason, class discussion of the activities for every topic is invaluable. Teachers are advised to spend class time discussing different ways to formulate problems and brainstorming possible approaches to their solution. Students need help in overcoming the misconception that in math there is always one exact answer and only one way to solve the problem. Teachers need to encourage and reward creativity and divergent thinking in these activities.

Teaching Suggestions by Topic

Part 1: Patterns

Mathematics is often defined as the *study of patterns.* Making students conscious of patterns can help them to see important relationships in mathematics. Number patterns are a nonthreatening way to help students learn about special number properties. Students should be encouraged to create their own patterns—both visual and numerical.

Organized counting dovetails nicely with pattern recognition. A student soon learns that multiplication is a shortcut to counting or adding. Breaking a problem into smaller parts may be easier than approaching it as a whole. Students should talk about the advantages and disadvantages of approaching a problem through the organized counting of patterns.

For exercises in which students are asked to continue a given pattern, there may be more than one solution. Teachers should not be too quick to assume that a student's answer is wrong just because it is different; examining that pattern may show that the student has discovered a perfectly good pattern of his or her own.

Part 2: Imagery

The ability to visualize is extremely helpful in solving problems. In the regular curriculum, students rarely have an opportunity to develop visual-thinking skills. In addition to providing much-needed practice, these lessons may serve as models for teachers who wish to create similar activities for further work in imagery and visual thinking.

Many of the activities in this section lend themselves to elaboration. Students should be encouraged to look for geometric shapes and visual patterns in their environment. They might bring in clippings from magazines and newspapers to illustrate such concepts as symmetry, congruence, rotation, and similarity. Most students enjoy creating their own designs that allow them to explore geometric relationships.

Part 3: Logic

For many students, the worksheets on logic will be more difficult than others in this book. Consequently, teachers are advised to take the additional time needed to explain the conventions of Venn diagrams and to provide model solutions. Students should be shown how to formulate their own questions, for this can enhance their understanding of the principles and structure of logic problems. Logic problems that seem overwhelmingly complex can often be simplified by breaking the problem into smaller problems. Students who do this will discover that taking one small step at a time can lead them to a solution.

You may need to give special attention to the terminology of Venn diagrams. Some students may be especially confused by the terms *both, and, either, or,* and *only.* For example, *in A and B* means "within the sections where A and B meet"; *either* means "in A or in B or in the section where A and b meet"; *in A only* means "in the portion of A that is not shared by any other shape." Examples are given in the text to clarify these terms.

Making Successful Thinkers and Problem Solvers

Students will see themselves as good problem solvers if they experience repeated success. Thus, when first introducing new critical thinking activities in any topic, it is better to err in selecting pages that are too easy than to have students struggle and conclude that they are unable to solve nonroutine problems. Through class discussion and work within small groups, students will have the chance to observe the thinking strategies of their peers. Eventually, they will muster the confidence to explore possible solution strategies on their own. At this point, they will be well on their way to becoming proficient critical thinkers in all their mathematics work.

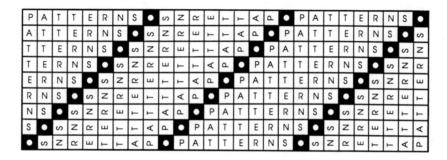

PART 1: PATTERNS

NUMBER PATTERNS ★

Find each pattern. Fill in the missing numbers in the row.

1.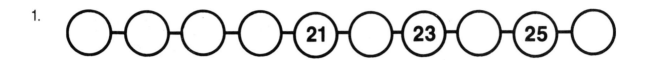
( ) ( ) ( ) ( ) (21) ( ) (23) ( ) (25) ( )

2.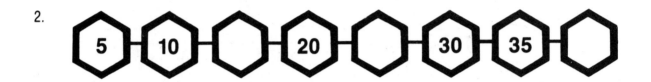
(5) (10) ( ) (20) ( ) (30) (35) ( )

3.
(9) (18) (27) ( ) (45) ( ) ( ) ( ) ( ) ( )

4.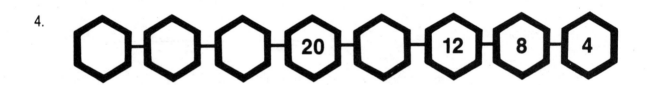
( ) ( ) ( ) (20) ( ) (12) (8) (4)

5.
( ) ( ) (56) (55) ( ) ( ) (52) ( ) ( ) ( )

6.
(1) (4) (7) (10) (13) ( ) ( ) ( )

7.
(1) (2) (2) (3) (3) (3) ( ) ( ) ( ) ( )

CRITICAL THINKING ACTIVITIES IN PATTERNS, IMAGERY, LOGIC   Dale Seymour Publications

SUM PATTERNS

Add the numbers two at a time, and write the sums in the circles and squares. Describe each pattern.

1.
| 1 | 2 | 3 | 4 | 5 | 6 | 7 | | |
(3) [5] ○ □ ○ □ ○ □ ○

Description: _____

2.
| 1 | 3 | 5 | 7 | 9 | 11 | | |
(4) [8] ○ □ ○ □ ○ □ ○

Description: _____

3.
| 2 | 4 | 6 | 8 | 10 | 12 | | |
○ □ ○ □ ○ □ ○ □ ○

Description: _____

4.
| 3 | 6 | 9 | 12 | 15 | 18 | | |
○ □ ○ □ ○ □ ○ □ ○

Description: _____

5.
| 1 | 4 | 9 | 16 | 25 | 36 | | |
○ □ ○ □ ○ □ ○ □ ○

Description: _____

6.
| 1 | 3 | 6 | 10 | 15 | 21 | | |
○ □ ○ □ ○ □ ○ □ ○

Description: _____

NUMBER PATTERNS

Complete the number patterns.

1.   2, 4, 6, _____, _____ , _____

2.   70, 60, 50, _____ , _____ , _____

3.   12, 15, _____, _____ , _____ , 27

Fill in the missing numbers. Look for a pattern that relates the number sentences.

4. $9 + 9 =$ _____   ↔ $9 \times 9 =$ _____

5. $24 + 3 =$ _____   ↔ $24 \times 3 =$ _____

6. a. $47 + 2 =$ _____   ↔ $47 \times 2 =$ _____

   b. $497 + 2 =$ _____   ↔ $497 \times 2 =$ _____

   c. $4997 + 2 =$ _____   ↔ $4997 \times 2 =$ _____

   d. _____ + ___ = _____   ↔   _____ × ___ = _____

   e. Describe the pattern. _____

Find the pattern to help you fill in the missing numbers.

7. a. $78 +$ $23 =$ _____   8. a. $12 -$ $11 =$ _____

   b. $778 +$ $223 =$ _____   b. $123 -$ $111 =$ _____

   c. $7778 +$ $2223 =$ _____   c. $1234 -$ $1111 =$ _____

   d. $77778 +$ $22223 =$ _____   d. $12345 -$ $11111 =$ _____

   e. _____ + _____ = _____   e. _____ - _____ = _____

   f. Describe the pattern: f. Describe the pattern:

   _____   _____

   _____   _____

PATTERNS IN A HUNDREDS CHART

Fill in the missing numbers in each chart.
What is the pattern of the missing numbers?

1	2	3	4	5	6	7	8		10
11	12	13	14	15	16	17		19	20
21	22	23	24	25	26		28	29	30
31	32	33	34	35		37	38	39	40
41	42	43	44		46	47	48	49	50
51	52	53		55	56	57	58	59	60
61	62		64	65	66	67	68	69	70
71		73	74	75	76	77	78	79	80
	82	83	84	85	86	87	88	89	
91	92	93	94	95	96	97	98		100

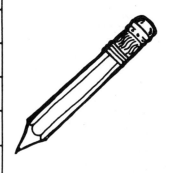

1. _____

1	2		4	5		7	8		10
11		13	14		16	17		19	20
	22	23		25	26		28	29	
31	32		34	35		37	38		40
41		43	44		46	47		49	50
	52	53		55	56		58	59	
61	62		64	65		67	68		70
71		73	74		76	77		79	80
	82	83		85	86		88	89	
91	92		94	95		97	98		100

2. _____

PATTERN STEPS

Draw the sequence of steps from the simplest to the most complex.
The first one is done as an example.

1.

2.

3.

4. Design a pattern of your own. Mix up the steps.
   Ask a classmate to put the steps in order.

CALENDAR PATTERNS

Calendars are filled with number patterns. Here is a 12-month calendar. Fill in the names of the missing months and the circled squares.

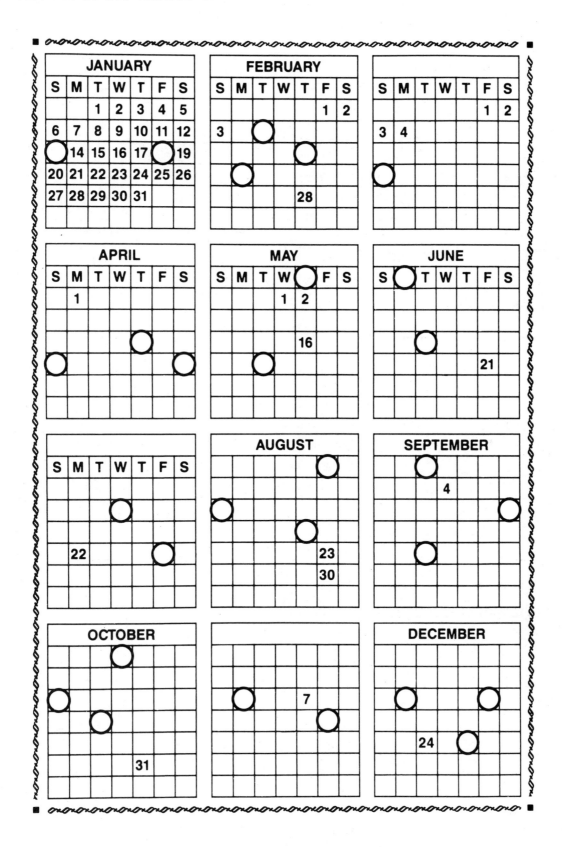

COMMON PROPERTY PATTERNS

Look at the numbers in each shape.
What do the numbers have in common?

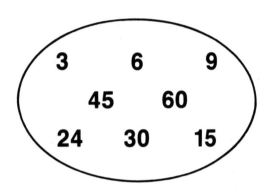

3   6   9
45   60
24   30   15

678   456
789   567
234   123

1. _____

_____

2. _____

_____

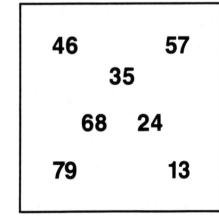

46   57
35
68   24
79   13

72   81
63   90
27   9   36
54   45
99   18

3. _____

_____

4. _____

_____

CRITICAL THINKING ACTIVITIES IN PATTERNS, IMAGERY, LOGIC   Dale Seymour Publications

PATTERNS IN SHAPES

Continue each pattern.

1.

2.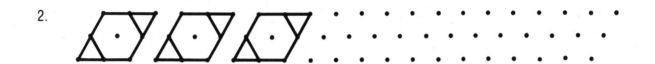

3.

4.

5.

EQUAL DISTANCE PATTERNS

Each number line below is divided into equal parts.
Fill in the missing numbers.

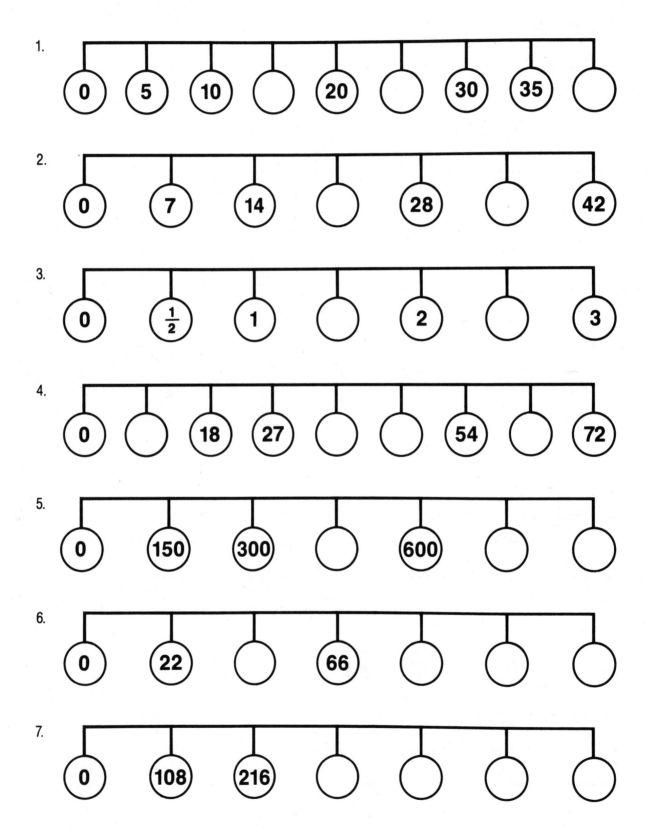

1. 0 5 10 ◯ 20 ◯ 30 35 ◯

2. 0 7 14 ◯ 28 ◯ 42

3. 0 ½ 1 ◯ 2 ◯ 3

4. 0 ◯ 18 27 ◯ ◯ 54 ◯ 72

5. 0 150 300 ◯ 600 ◯ ◯

6. 0 22 ◯ 66 ◯ ◯ ◯

7. 0 108 216 ◯ ◯ ◯ ◯

CRITICAL THINKING ACTIVITIES IN PATTERNS, IMAGERY, LOGIC   Dale Seymour Publications

NICKEL AND DIME PATTERNS

What different combinations of nickels and dimes make each given amount?

Example A

TOTAL 35¢

Number of Nickels	1	3	5	7
Number of Dimes	3	2	1	0

Example B

TOTAL 40¢

Number of Nickels	0	2	4	6	8
Number of Dimes	4	3	2	1	0

1. TOTAL 45¢

Number of Nickels	1	3			
Number of Dimes	4	3			

2. TOTAL 50¢

Number of Nickels	0				
Number of Dimes	5				

3. TOTAL 55¢

Number of Nickels	1	3			
Number of Dimes	5				

4. TOTAL 60¢

Number of Nickels	0						
Number of Dimes	6						

5. Describe the patterns you discovered.

_____

_____

_____

NUMBER TABLE PATTERNS

Find each pattern. Then complete the table and rule.

1.

1	2	3	4	5	6	7
↓	↓	↓	↓	↓	↓	↓
2	3	4	5	__	__	__

Rule:
Add 1.

2.

1	2	3	4	5	6	7
↓	↓	↓	↓	↓	↓	↓
9	10	11	12	__	__	__

Rule:

_____

3.

1	2	3	4	5	6	7
↓	↓	↓	↓	↓	↓	↓
3	6	9	__	__	__	__

Rule:

_____

4.

10	11	12	13	14	15	16
↓	↓	↓	↓	↓	↓	↓
3	4	5	__	__	__	__

Rule:

_____

5.

5	1	3	6	7	2	4
↓	↓	↓	↓	↓	↓	↓
30	6	__	__	__	__	__

Rule:

_____

CRITICAL THINKING ACTIVITIES IN PATTERNS, IMAGERY, LOGIC   Dale Seymour Publications

LETTER COMBINATION PATTERNS

How many different words can you form when you read the letter triangle from left to right? Write the words.

Example:
```
    N
   /
A
   \
    T
```
2 words: __AN__   __AT__

	Number of Words	**Word List**

1.
```
    N
   /
O
   \
    F
```
_____ words: _____

2.
```
    F
   /
I
   \
    T
```
_____ words: _____

3.
```
       T
      /
     O
    /  \
D        N
    \  /
     A
      \
       B
```
_____ words: _____

4.
```
       T
      /
     I
    /  \
B        G
    \  /
     A
      \
       D
```
_____ words: _____

How many four-letter combinations are possible?
Not all combinations are words.

5.

_____ combinations: _____

_____

6.
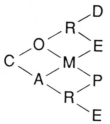
_____ combinations: _____

_____

7.   If you had a letter triangle that used five levels of letters, how many different five-letter combinations would be possible? _____

8.   Design your own letter triangle that makes as many three-letter words as possible.

DESIGN PATTERNS

Continue each pattern.

1.

2.

3.

CRITICAL THINKING ACTIVITIES IN PATTERNS, IMAGERY, LOGIC   Dale Seymour Publications

ATTRIBUTE PATTERNS

Look for a pattern. Extend your pattern by drawing three
or more figures. Use only the figures in the box.

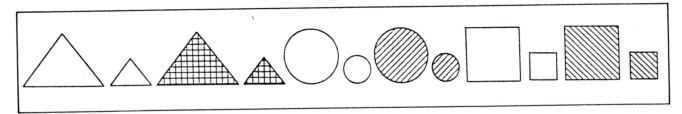

1. 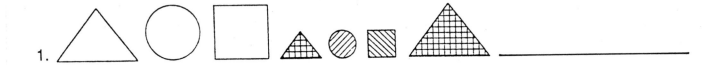 _____

2. 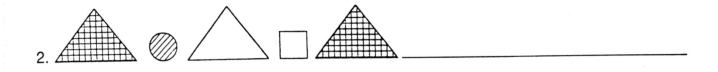 _____

3.  _____

4.  _____

5. 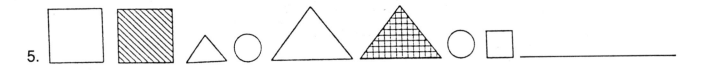 _____

6. 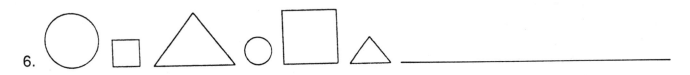 _____

7. Design your own pattern below. Ask a classmate to describe the
pattern and extend it.

_____

NUMBER TABLE PATTERNS

Find each pattern. Then complete the table and rule.

1.

1	2	3	4	5	6	7
↓	↓	↓	↓	↓	↓	↓
8	9	10	—	—	—	—

Rule:
Add 7.

2.

15	16	17	18	19	20	21
↓	↓	↓	↓	↓	↓	↓
18	19	20	—	—	—	—

Rule:
_____

3.

35	34	33	32	31	30	29
↓	↓	↓	↓	↓	↓	↓
25	24	23	—	—	—	—

Rule:
_____

4.

4	9	3	12	15	6	100
↓	↓	↓	↓	↓	↓	↓
9	14	—	—	—	—	—

Rule:
_____

5.

3	5	7	10	11	14	20
↓	↓	↓	↓	↓	↓	↓
9	15	—	—	—	—	—

Rule:
_____

CRITICAL THINKING ACTIVITIES IN PATTERNS, IMAGERY, LOGIC   Dale Seymour Publications

NUMBER PATTERNS

Find each pattern. Fill in the missing numbers.

1. 2, 4, ___, 8, ___, 12, ___, ___, ___, ___

2. 3, 6, ___, ___, 15, ___, ___, ___, ___, ___

3. 17, 27, ___, 47, ___, ___, ___, ___, ___, ___, ___

4. ___, ___, ___, ___, 21, 23, 25, ___, ___, ___, ___

5. 11, ___, 33, ___, 55, 66, ___, ___, ___, ___

6. ___, 85, 80, 75, 70, ___, ___, ___, ___, ___

7. 101, ___, 303, ___, ___, ___, 707, ___, ___, ___, ___

8. 12, 23, 34, ___, ___, ___, ___, ___, ___, ___, ___

9. 1, 8, 15, 22, 29, 36, ___, ___, ___, ___

10. 7, 16, 25, 34, 43, ___, ___, ___, ___, ___

CALENDAR PATTERNS

Here is a 12-month calendar. Most of the numbers, days, and months are missing. Fill in the names of the missing months. Fill in the circled squares.

JANUARY
S	M	T	W	T	F	S
			1	2	3	4
5	6	7	○			
					○	

FEBRUARY
S	M	T	W	T	F	S
						1
2	3					
	○				○	

MARCH
S	M	T	W	T	F	S
						1
			○			8
						15
○						22
						29

APRIL
S	M	T	W	T	F	S
		1				
			9			○
○				17		
					25	

MAY
S	M	T	W	T	F	S
					○	
				1		
		7				
	13				○	

JUNE
S	M	T	W	T	F	S
						○
					○	
	○					
22	23	24	25	26	27	28

JULY
S	M	T	W	T	F	S
Ⓢ						
		2				
				○		
	○					

(month)
			○			
					16	
	○					

(month)
					○	
						○
			18			
						○

(month)
	○					
				○	4	
	○					
				31		

(month)
					○	
	3					
		○				
			○			

(month)
		○			○	

CRITICAL THINKING ACTIVITIES IN PATTERNS, IMAGERY, LOGIC   Dale Seymour Publications

HUNDREDS CHART PATTERNS

Fill in the missing numbers in each chart.
What is the pattern of the missing numbers?

1	2	3	4	5		7	8	9	10
11		13	14	15	16	17		19	20
21	22	23		25	26	27	28	29	
31	32	33	34	35		37	38	39	40
41		43	44	45	46	47		49	50
51	52	53		55	56	57	58	59	
61	62	63	64	65		67	68	69	70
71		73	74	75	76	77		79	80
81	82	83		85	86	87	88	89	
91	92	93	94	95		97	98	99	100

1. _____

1	2	3	4	5	6		8	9	10
11	12	13		15	16	17	18	19	20
	22	23	24	25	26	27		29	30
31	32	33	34		36	37	38	39	40
41		43	44	45	46	47	48		50
51	52	53	54	55		57	58	59	60
61	62		64	65	66	67	68	69	
71	72	73	74	75	76		78	79	80
81	82	83		85	86	87	88	89	90
	92	93	94	95	96	97		99	100

2. _____

EVEN AND ODD PATTERNS

Even and odd numbers can be arranged in dot patterns.
These patterns have certain shapes.

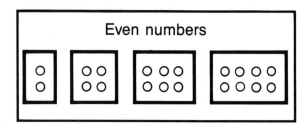

Even numbers

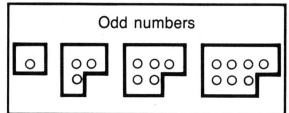

Odd numbers

The sum of two odd numbers is always even.
Divide the even dot patterns below into two odd-number parts.

Examples:

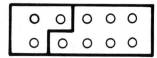

1.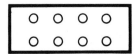

2.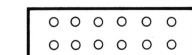

3.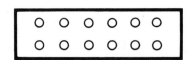

4.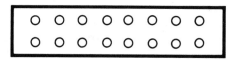

The sum of any two even numbers is always an _____ number.
Divide the even dot patterns below into two even-number parts.

5.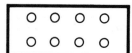

6.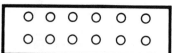

7.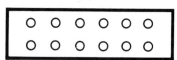

8.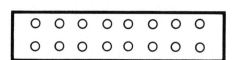

9. From the examples above, what is the sum of two even numbers?

_____

10. What is the sum of an odd and an even number? _____

CRITICAL THINKING ACTIVITIES IN PATTERNS, IMAGERY, LOGIC   Dale Seymour Publications

SUM PATTERNS

Add the numbers three at a time, and write the sums in the circles and squares. Describe each pattern.

1.

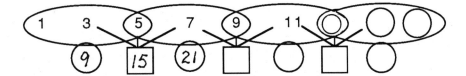

Description: _____

2.

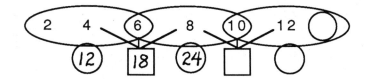

Description: _____

3.

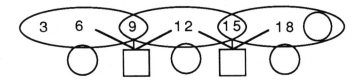

Description: _____

4.

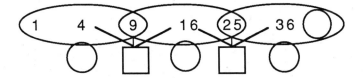

Description: _____

5.

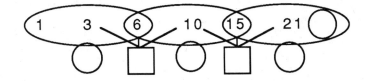

Description: _____

6.

Description: _____

7. Go back and extend patterns 5 and 6.

DESIGN PATTERNS

Continue each pattern.

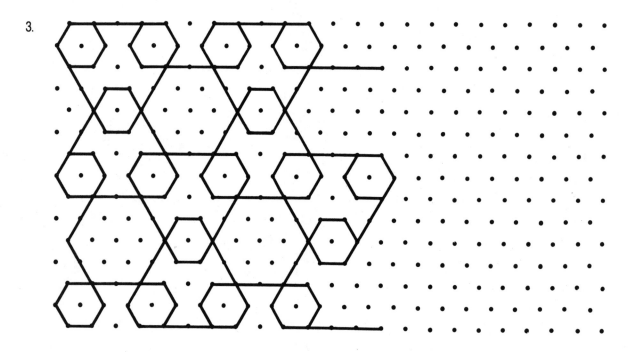

1.

2.

3.

DOT AND NUMBER PATTERNS

1. Sketch the next two dot figures in the pattern below. Count the dots in each figure and record your answer. Extend the number pattern.

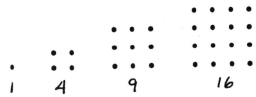

1   4   9   16

2. Describe the number pattern. _____

3. Does this number pattern continue? _____
   Try another figure to see.

4. Use your results to fill in the missing numbers in the following pattern. For each step, write the number of dots added to the previous figure.

    1

    4   = 1 + 3

    9   = 1 + 3 + ___

    16 = 1 + 3 + ___ + ___

    ____ = ___ + ___ + ___ + ___ + ___

    ____ = ___ + ___ + ___ + ___ + ___ + ___

5. Sketch the next three dot triangles in the pattern below. Count the dots in each figure and record your answer. Extend the number pattern.

1   3   6   10

6. Use your results to fill in the missing numbers in the following pattern.

    1

    3   = 1 + 2

    6   = 1 + 2 + ___

    10 = ___ + ___ + ___ + ___

    ____ = ___ + ___ + ___ + ___ + ___

    ____ = ___ + ___ + ___ + ___ + ___ + ___

7. Describe this pattern. _____

DIGIT COMBINATION PATTERNS

How many different numbers can you form when you read the number triangle from left to right?

Example: 1 < 2 / 3   2 numbers: __12__   __13__

1. 2 < 3 / 5   ____ numbers   2. 3 ⟨ 5 < 7 / 2 ⟩ 6 < 1   ____ numbers

Number List: _____   Number List: _____

3. 4 ⟨ 5 < 1 / 2 ⟩ 6 < 8   ____ numbers   4. 1 ⟨ 3 < 7 < 9 / 6 ⟩ 2 < 5 / 4 ⟩ 8 < 0   ____ numbers

Number List: _____   Number List: _____

5. 9 ⟨ 8 < 6 < 3 / 2 ⟩ 5 < 1 / 7 ⟩ 4 < 0   ____ numbers   6. 1 ⟨ 4 < 6 < 8 < 5 / 7 ⟩ 5 / 2 ⟩ 0 ⟩ 3 / 9 ⟩ 1 ⟩ 2 < 3 / 4   ____ numbers

Number List: _____   Number List: _____

7. Summarize your results by completing the table.

How many digits in each number?	2	3	4	5	6	7	8
How many numbers?	2	4					

PRODUCT PATTERNS

Study this multiplication pattern. Note the longest row has two times as many digits as each factor. Check the answer.

```
        444
      × 444
         16
       1616
     161616
       1616
     +  16
     197136
```

See if the pattern shown above gives the correct answers for the problems below. Hint: Write 1 × 1 as 01.

1.
```
      11
    × 11
      01
    0101
    + 01
```

2.
```
      111
    × 111
```

3.
```
      1111
    × 1111
```

4.
```
      55
    × 55
```

5.
```
      555
    × 555
```

6.
```
      5555
    × 5555
```

7.
```
      44
    × 33
      12
    1212
    + 12
```

8.
```
      444
    × 333
       12
     1212
   121212
     1212
   +  12
```

9. Try to discover and describe why this pattern works. Hint: Look at each multiplication pattern and observe that the zeros have been omitted.

COMMON PROPERTY PATTERNS

Look at the numbers in each shape.
What do the numbers have in common?

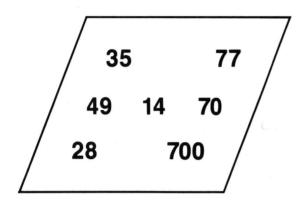

35   77
49 14 70
28   700

33   434
15,751
77   101

1. _____

2. _____

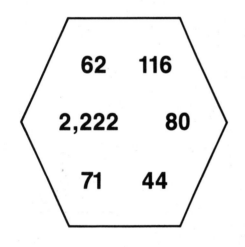

62   116
2,222   80
71   44

84
60   48
108
96   12

3. _____

4. _____

PRODUCT PATTERNS

1. Describe a pattern for the numbers in row 4.

   _____

2. Describe a pattern for the numbers in column 5.

   _____

3. Describe a pattern for the numbers in the corner of each "backwards L" section.

   _____

COLUMN

	1	2	3	4	5	6	7
	1	2	3	4	5	6	7
	2	4	6	8	10	12	14
R	3	6	9	12	15	18	21
O	4	8	12	16	20	24	28
W	5	10	15	20	25	30	35
	6	12	18	24	30	36	42
	7	14	21	28	35	42	49

4. Describe a pattern for the sum of the numbers in each "backwards L" section.

   _____

5. Describe the pattern relationship between any four numbers in a square position. For example: ⊞

   _____

6. In any row the sum of the number in column _____ and the number in

   column _____ equals the number in column _____ . Is there more than

   one solution to this problem? _____ If so, name one: _____

   _____

7. What other patterns can you discover? _____

   _____

EVEN AND ODD PATTERNS

Five in a row makes a BINGO.
Mark a BINGO of odd numbers by putting an X on each.
Mark a BINGO of even numbers by drawing a ring around each.

1.

B	I	N	G	O
7	18	40	60	72
11	29	33	58	67
9	17	free	52	65
6	23	35	50	73
3	25	41	49	61

2.

B	I	N	G	O
11	20	34	52	66
6	28	37	60	61
2	18	free	55	72
10	24	44	48	70
14	25	38	56	64

3.

B	I	N	G	O
7	18	41	55	67
3	21	35	48	71
15	29	free	59	72
6	27	44	49	65
1	23	33	60	73

CRITICAL THINKING ACTIVITIES IN PATTERNS, IMAGERY, LOGIC   Dale Seymour Publications

SPECIAL NUMBER PATTERNS

Use a calculator to help you discover the number patterns below.
Fill in the missing numbers, then describe each pattern.

1. $1089 \times 1 =$ _____

   $1089 \times 2 =$ _____

   $1089 \times 3 =$ _____

   $1089 \times 4 =$ _____

   $1089 \times 5 =$ _____

   $1089 \times 6 =$ _____

   $1089 \times 7 =$ _____

   $1089 \times 8 =$ _____

   Description: _____

   _____

2. $1 \times 8 + 1 =$ _____

   $12 \times 8 + 2 =$ _____

   $123 \times 8 + 3 =$ _____

   $1234 \times 8 + 4 =$ _____

   $12345 \times 8 + 5 =$ _____

   $123456 \times 8 + 6 =$ _____

   $1234567 \times 8 + 7 =$ _____

   $12345678 \times 8 + 8 =$ _____

   Description: _____

   _____

3. $3367 \times 33 =$ _____

   $3367 \times 66 =$ _____

   $3367 \times 99 =$ _____

   $3367 \times 132 =$ _____

   $3367 \times 165 =$ _____

   $3367 \times 198 =$ _____

   $3367 \times 231 =$ _____

   Description: _____

   _____

4. $1 \times 9 + 2 =$ _____

   $12 \times 9 + 3 =$ _____

   $123 \times 9 + 4 =$ _____

   $1234 \times 9 + 5 =$ _____

   $12345 \times 9 + 6 =$ _____

   $123456 \times 9 + 7 =$ _____

   $1234567 \times 9 + 8 =$ _____

   Description: _____

   _____

5. In problem 4, does it matter whether you multiply or add first? _____

   Which is correct? _____

NUMBER PATTERNS

★★★

Find each pattern. Fill in the missing numbers in the row.

1. (6)—(12)—(18)—(24)—( )—( )—( )—( )—( )

2. [18][25][32][39][ ][ ][ ][ ][ ][ ]

3. ( )—(97)—(95)—(93)—( )—( )—( )—( )—( )

4. [7][ ][ ][28][35][ ][ ][ ][ ][ ]

5. (101)—(212)—(323)—( )—( )—( )—( )—( )

6. [19][28][37][ ][ ][ ][ ][ ][ ][ ]

7. (1)—(2)—(4)—(8)—(16)—( )—( )—( )

8. [10][20][40][70][110][ ][ ][ ][ ][ ]

CRITICAL THINKING ACTIVITIES IN PATTERNS, IMAGERY, LOGIC   Dale Seymour Publications

ADDEND PATTERNS

Write all the possible sums for each counting number below, using exactly two addends (including zero). Count the number of possible sums.

Counting Number		Possible Sums (2 addends)	Number of 2-Addend Sums
0	=	0 + 0	1
1	=	0 + 1	1
2	=	0 + 2 = 1 + 1	2
3	=	0 + 3 = 1 + 2	2
4	=	0 + 4 = 1 + 3 = ___ + ___	3
5	=		
6	=		
7	=		
8	=		
9	=		
10	=		

Without writing out the sums, complete the table below.

Counting Number	14	15	16	17 ·	· 20	21 ·	· 50 ·	· 100
Number of 2-Addend Sums								

Describe a rule for even numbers. _____

Describe a rule for odd numbers. _____

WINNING PATTERNS

In round 1, player 6 wins the match against player 1.
Round 2 begins. Player 6 then plays the winner of
the match between players 8 and 3.
Study the numbers and find out who wins each
match. Then look at the number pattern determined
by the winners.

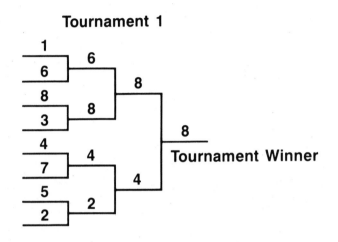

Tournament 1

1. Describe a number pattern that determines the winner.

_____

Now do the same for Tournament 2.

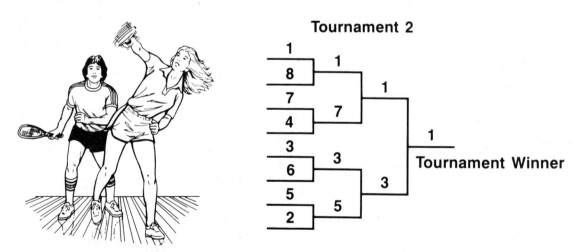

Tournament 2

2. Describe a number pattern that determines the winner.

_____

CALENDAR PATTERNS

Here is a 12-month calendar. Most of the numbers, days, and months are missing. Fill in the names of the missing months. Fill in the circled squares.

LETTER COMBINATION PATTERNS

Read each letter triangle from left to right. Use a different path to spell the *same* words. Circling the paths may help you find how many there are.

Example: <u>4</u> paths

1. D [OENNE triangle] _____ paths

2. T [OO triangle] _____ paths

3. T [ONNN triangle] _____ paths

4. T [OENNEE triangle] _____ paths

5. T [OESNNEE triangle] _____ paths

6. Make a letter puzzle of your first name.
    How many paths can you take to spell it? _____

7. Summarize your results by completing the table.

Number of letters in each word	2	3	4	5	6	7	8
Number of paths	2	4					

CRITICAL THINKING ACTIVITIES IN PATTERNS, IMAGERY, LOGIC   Dale Seymour Publications

PATTERNS AND RULES

Find each pattern. Then complete the table and rule.

1.

5	6	7	8	9	10	11
↓	↓	↓	↓	↓	↓	↓
14	15	16	__	__	__	__

Rule:
Add 9.

2.

13	20	15	7	12	50	100
↓	↓	↓	↓	↓	↓	↓
9	16	__	__	__	__	__

Rule:

_____

3.

5	17	9	11	25	31	100
↓	↓	↓	↓	↓	↓	↓
10	34	18	__	__	__	__

Rule:

_____

4.

9	5	15	8	11	13	100
↓	↓	↓	↓	↓	↓	↓
45	25	75	__	__	__	__

Rule:

_____

5.

1	2	3	4	5	6	7
↓	↓	↓	↓	↓	↓	↓
3	5	7	9	__	__	__

Rule:

_____

_____

COUNTING SQUARES PATTERNS

How many squares are in each figure? You can combine small squares to make larger squares. Write your answers in the chart below.

1 × 1	2 × 2	3 × 3	4 × 4	5 × 5	6 × 6

1.

Size of Square	Number of Squares With:						Total Number of Squares
	1- Square Unit	4- Square Unit	9- Square Unit	16- Square Unit	25- Square Unit	36- Square Unit	
1 × 1	1						1
2 × 2	4	1					5
3 × 3	9	4	1				14
4 × 4	_____	_____	_____	_____			_____
5 × 5	_____	_____	_____	_____	_____		_____
6 × 6	_____	_____	_____	_____	_____	_____	_____

2. Describe the patterns you found. _____

_____

3. Explain how you could use this pattern to count the squares in a 10 × 10 figure.

_____

_____

CRITICAL THINKING ACTIVITIES IN PATTERNS, IMAGERY, LOGIC   Dale Seymour Publications

COMMON PROPERTY PATTERNS

Look at the number in each shape.
What do the numbers have in common?

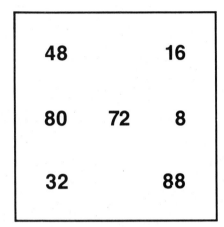

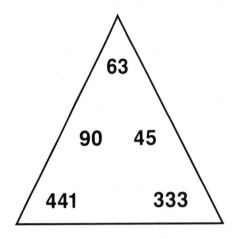

1. _____

_____

_____

2. _____

_____

_____

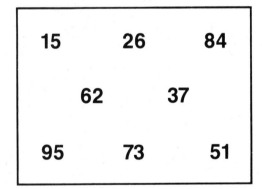

3. _____

_____

_____

4. _____

_____

_____

PAPER STRIP PATTERNS

1. a. Cut a strip of paper, then draw a dotted line in the middle.

    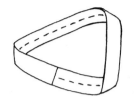

    b. Tape the ends together after making *one* twist.

    c. Cut the loop along the dotted line.

    d. What do you get? One large loop, one small loop, or two loops? _____

2. Now cut a strip of paper and draw two dotted lines on it.
    Follow the directions above for making a twisted loop.
    Remember to twist your paper once before you tape the ends
    together. Then cut along both dotted lines. Describe your results.

    _____

3. Make another twisted loop with three dotted lines.
    Cut along all three lines. Describe your results.

    _____

4. Cut another strip of paper and draw four dotted lines
    on it. Twist the strip and tape the ends together.
    Cut along all four lines. Describe your results.

    _____

5. Make a loop with five dotted lines. Cut along all five
    lines and describe your results.

    _____

6. Predict the pattern and complete the chart below. Make and cut
    loops to verify your predictions.

Number of Cuts	1	2	3	4	5	6	7	8
Number of Large Loops	1	1	2	2	3	3	4	4
Number of Small Loops	0	1	0	1				

DESIGN PATTERNS

Continue each pattern.

1.

2.

3.

NUMBER PATTERNS

Mathematics is often defined as the study of pattern. Some number patterns are started below. Look for a pattern. When you find one, extend it . Fill in the blanks with your numbers, then describe the patterns in words.

1. 1976, 1980, 1984, _____ , _____ , _____

    Description: _____

2. 91, 82, 73, _____ , _____ , _____ , _____ , _____ , _____

    Description: _____

3. 1, 10, 100, _____ , _____ , _____

    Description: _____

4. 37, 41, 45, 49, _____ , _____ , _____ , _____

    Description: _____

5. 121, 232, 343, _____ , _____ , _____

    Description: _____

6. 117, 126, 135, 144, 153, _____ , _____ , _____ , _____

    Description: _____

7. 12, 24, 36, 48, 510, _____ , _____ , _____

    Description: _____

8. 1, 4, 9, 16, _____ , _____ , _____ , _____

    Description: _____

9. 1, 8, 27, _____ , _____ , _____

    Description: _____

10. 1, 3, 6, 10, 15, _____ , _____ , _____

    Description: _____

 CRITICAL THINKING ACTIVITIES IN PATTERNS, IMAGERY, LOGIC   Dale Seymour Publications

BINGO PATTERNS

Five in a row make a BINGO.
Mark a BINGO of numbers whose digits total 7. Draw a line through them.
Mark a BINGO of numbers whose digits differ by 2. Put an X on each.
Mark a BINGO of square numbers by drawing a ring around each.

1.

B	I	N	G	O
10	20	42	53	70
7	25	43	52	75
9	16	free	49	64
12	22	34	57	61
13	24	35	46	68

2.

B	I	N	G	O
4	18	42	46	61
13	24	35	52	68
10	20	free	49	64
12	16	34	57	75
7	25	43	53	70

3.

B	I	N	G	O
4	25	42	57	64
9	24	46	53	73
10	18	free	50	68
13	20	31	46	75
2	30	49	48	70

ERROR PATTERNS

Help the teacher by finding the error pattern in each student's work below. Each problem in a set has the same error pattern. Do the remaining problems the way each student would have done them. Then write a description of the pattern.

1.
```
  36      47      36      82      14      39
 +19     +29     +45     +59     +38     +47
  45      66      71     131    ┌────┐  ┌────┐
                              │    │  │    │
                              └────┘  └────┘
```

Description: _____

_____

2.
```
   42     521     265     592     365     472
  -19    -173    -182    -278    -189    -148
   37     452     123     326   ┌────┐  ┌────┐
                                │    │  │    │
                                └────┘  └────┘
```

Description: _____

_____

3.
```
  307    8006    9305     602    5004    7003
 -149   -2347   -3028    -213   -2329   -2148
   68    3769    6187     299   ┌────┐  ┌────┐
                               │    │  │    │
                               └────┘  └────┘
```

Description: _____

_____

4.
```
   37      48      52      69      56      76
 × 6     × 5     × 7     × 3     × 4     × 8
 1842    2040    3514    1827   ┌────┐  ┌────┐
                               │    │  │    │
                               └────┘  └────┘
```

Description: _____

_____

LOGIC PATTERNS

1. Write at least one number, if possible, in each of the seven sections.

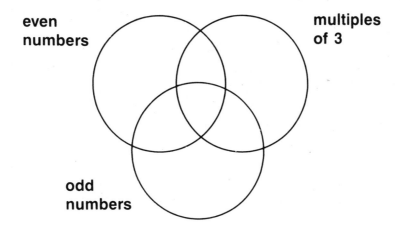

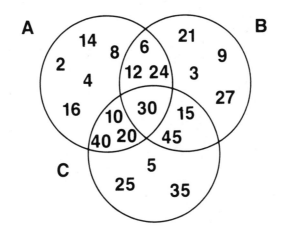

2. Describe set A. _____

3. Describe set B. _____

4. Describe set C. _____

5. Describe the intersection of B and C. _____

_____

6. Describe the intersection of A and C. _____

_____

7. Describe the intersection of A and B and C. _____

_____

PATTERN SEARCH

1. Which digit does not appear twice in any column, row, or diagonal? _____

2. What two-digit number appears in every row?_____

3. In the entire number grid, the largest:

    a. two-digit odd number is _____ in row _____ .

    b. three-digit even number is _____ in row _____ .

    c. four-digit odd number is _____ in row _____ .

    d. five-digit even number is _____ in row _____ .

    e. six-digit odd number is _____ in row _____ .

    f. seven-digit even number is_____ in row _____ .

    g. eight-digit odd number is _____ in row _____ .

    h. nine-digit even number is_____ in row _____ .

	J	K	L	M	N	O	P	Q	R	S
A	1	3	0	8	4	6	9	2	5	7
B	0	2	5	7	9	1	3	8	6	4
C	5	9	1	3	6	8	4	0	2	7
D	6	0	9	8	7	4	2	5	1	3
E	2	5	6	7	0	8	1	3	4	9
F	8	1	3	9	5	7	0	6	4	2
G	9	4	7	1	3	2	5	6	8	0
H	2	4	9	0	7	6	1	3	8	5
I	9	7	2	5	6	0	8	1	3	4
J	4	1	3	6	7	5	8	2	0	9

4. Find a two-digit square number in every row.

    Row A: _____   Row B: _____   Row C: _____   Row D: _____   Row E: _____

    Row F: _____   Row G: _____   Row H: _____   Row I: _____   Row J: _____

5. Find a two-digit multiple of 7 in these rows.

    Row A: _____   Row B: _____   Row C: _____   Row D: _____   Row E: _____

    Row F: _____   Row G: _____   Row H: _____   Row I: _____

6. What is the product of all the digits in each row?_____
   Why is it the same for each row?_____

7. A palindromic number is one that reads the same forwards and backwards, such as 565. What is the largest palindromic number you can find in the number grid above, using numbers that lie on a diagonal?_____

8. Describe some interesting number patterns that you discovered in the number grid.

   _____

CRITICAL THINKING ACTIVITIES IN PATTERNS, IMAGERY, LOGIC   Dale Seymour Publications

NUMBER CHAIN PATTERNS

Use a colored pencil or pen to draw the number chains in the grids below.

A *diagonal number chain* connects squares that share only a vertex (corner).

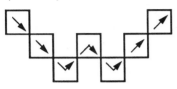

An *edge number chain* connects squares that share an edge.

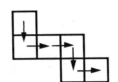

A *combined number chain* connects squares that share an edge or vertex.

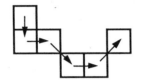

1. Find a diagonal chain of odd numbers that travels from one side of the square to the other.

	J	K	L	M	N	O	P	Q	R	S
A	1	3	0	8	4	6	9	2	5	7
B	0	2	5	7	9	1	3	8	6	4
C	5	9	1	3	6	8	4	0	2	7
D	6	0	9	8	7	4	2	5	1	3
E	2	5	6	7	0	8	1	3	4	9
F	8	1	3	9	5	7	0	6	4	2
G	9	4	7	1	3	2	5	6	8	0
H	2	4	9	0	7	6	1	3	8	5
I	9	7	2	5	6	0	8	1	3	4
J	4	1	3	6	7	5	8	2	0	9

2. Find a diagonal chain of even numbers that travels from one side of the square to the other.

	J	K	L	M	N	O	P	Q	R	S
A	1	3	0	8	4	6	9	2	5	7
B	0	2	5	7	9	1	3	8	6	4
C	5	9	1	3	6	8	4	0	2	7
D	6	0	9	8	7	4	2	5	1	3
E	2	5	6	7	0	8	1	3	4	9
F	8	1	3	9	5	7	0	6	4	2
G	9	4	7	1	3	2	5	6	8	0
H	2	4	9	0	7	6	1	3	8	5
I	9	7	2	5	6	0	8	1	3	4
J	4	1	3	6	7	5	8	2	0	9

3. Find a diagonal chain of odd numbers that travels from the top of the square to the bottom.

	J	K	L	M	N	O	P	Q	R	S
A	1	3	0	8	4	6	9	2	5	7
B	0	2	5	7	9	1	3	8	6	4
C	5	9	1	3	6	8	4	0	2	7
D	6	0	9	8	7	4	2	5	1	3
E	2	5	6	7	0	8	1	3	4	9
F	8	1	3	9	5	7	0	6	4	2
G	9	4	7	1	3	2	5	6	8	0
H	2	4	9	0	7	6	1	3	8	5
I	9	7	2	5	6	0	8	1	3	4
J	4	1	3	6	7	5	8	2	0	9

4. Find a diagonal chain of even numbers that travels from the top of the square to the bottom.

	J	K	L	M	N	O	P	Q	R	S
A	1	3	0	8	4	6	9	2	5	7
B	0	2	5	7	9	1	3	8	6	4
C	5	9	1	3	6	8	4	0	2	7
D	6	0	9	8	7	4	2	5	1	3
E	2	5	6	7	0	8	1	3	4	9
F	8	1	3	9	5	7	0	6	4	2
G	9	4	7	1	3	2	5	6	8	0
H	2	4	9	0	7	6	1	3	8	5
I	9	7	2	5	6	0	8	1	3	4
J	4	1	3	6	7	5	8	2	0	9

5. Using a combined number chain, what is the longest palindromic number you can locate in the square? _____

6. Using a combined number chain, what is the largest six-digit number you can locate in the square? _____

SPECIAL NUMBER PATTERNS

1. An interesting arithmetic pattern is shown below. It was developed by an Italian mathematician named Niccolo Tartaglia, who lived about 400 years ago. Check that all the statements are true, then extend the pattern.

    $1 + 2 = 3$

    $4 + 5 + 6 = 7 + 8$

    $9 + 10 + 11 + 12 = 13 + 14 + 15$

    $16 + 17 + 18 + 19 + 20 = \underline{\quad} + \underline{\quad} + \underline{\quad} + \underline{\quad}$

    $\underline{\quad} + \underline{\quad} + \underline{\quad} + \underline{\quad} + \underline{\quad} + \underline{\quad} = \underline{\quad} + \underline{\quad} + \underline{\quad} + \underline{\quad} + \underline{\quad}$

    $\underline{\quad} + \underline{\quad} + \underline{\quad} + \underline{\quad} + \underline{\quad} + \underline{\quad} + \underline{\quad} = \underline{\quad} + \underline{\quad} + \underline{\quad} + \underline{\quad} + \underline{\quad} + \underline{\quad}$

    Describe the pattern in one or more sentences: _____

    _____

2. Here is another of Niccolo Tartaglia's patterns. Extend the pattern. Hint: Remember that 1^2 means 1×1, 2^2 means 2×2, and so on.

    $1^2 = (2 \times 1 - 1)^2 = 1$

    $3^2 = (2 \times 2 - 1)^2 = 2 + 3 + 4$

    $5^2 = (2 \times 3 - 1)^2 = 3 + 4 + 5 + 6 + 7$

    $7^2 = (2 \times 4 - 1)^2 = \underline{\quad} + \underline{\quad} + \underline{\quad} + \underline{\quad} + \underline{\quad} + \underline{\quad} + \underline{\quad}$

    $9^2 = (\underline{\ } \times \underline{\ } - \underline{\ })^2 = \underline{\quad} + \underline{\quad} + \underline{\quad} + \underline{\quad} + \underline{\quad} + \underline{\quad} + \underline{\quad} + \underline{\quad} + \underline{\quad}$

    $11^2 = (\underline{\ } \times \underline{\ } - \underline{\ })^2 = \underline{\quad} + \underline{\quad} + \underline{\quad} + \underline{\quad} + \underline{\quad} + \underline{\quad} + \underline{\quad} + \underline{\quad} + \underline{\quad} + \underline{\quad} + \underline{\quad}$

    Describe the pattern in one or more sentences: _____

    _____

HUNDREDS CHART

1	2	3	4	5	6	7	8	9	10
11	12	13	14	15	16	17	18	19	20
21	22	23	24	25	26	27	28	29	30
31	32	33	34	35	36	37	38	39	40
41	42	43	44	45	46	47	48	49	50
51	52	53	54	55	56	57	58	59	60
61	62	63	64	65	66	67	68	69	70
71	72	73	74	75	76	77	78	79	80
81	82	83	84	85	86	87	88	89	90
91	92	93	94	95	96	97	98	99	100

NUMBER CHART

0	1	2	3	4	5	6	7	8	9
10	11	12	13	14	15	16	17	18	19
20	21	22	23	24	25	26	27	28	29
30	31	32	33	34	35	36	37	38	39
40	41	42	43	44	45	46	47	48	49
50	51	52	53	54	55	56	57	58	59
60	61	62	63	64	65	66	67	68	69
70	71	72	73	74	75	76	77	78	79
80	81	82	83	84	85	86	87	88	89
90	91	92	93	94	95	96	97	98	99

CRITICAL THINKING ACTIVITIES IN PATTERNS, IMAGERY, LOGIC   Dale Seymour Publications

ADDITION TABLE

+	1	2	3	4	5	6	7	8	9
1	2	3	4	5	6	7	8	9	10
2	3	4	5	6	7	8	9	10	11
3	4	5	6	7	8	9	10	11	12
4	5	6	7	8	9	10	11	12	13
5	6	7	8	9	10	11	12	13	14
6	7	8	9	10	11	12	13	14	15
7	8	9	10	11	12	13	14	15	16
8	9	10	11	12	13	14	15	16	17
9	10	11	12	13	14	15	16	17	18

MULTIPLICATION TABLE

×	1	2	3	4	5	6	7	8	9
1	1	2	3	4	5	6	7	8	9
2	2	4	6	8	10	12	14	16	18
3	3	6	9	12	15	18	21	24	27
4	4	8	12	16	20	24	28	32	36
5	5	10	15	20	25	30	35	40	45
6	6	12	18	24	30	36	42	48	54
7	7	14	21	28	35	42	49	56	63
8	8	16	24	32	40	48	56	64	72
9	9	18	27	36	45	54	63	72	81

CRITICAL THINKING ACTIVITIES IN PATTERNS, IMAGERY, LOGIC   Dale Seymour Publications

PASCAL'S TRIANGLE

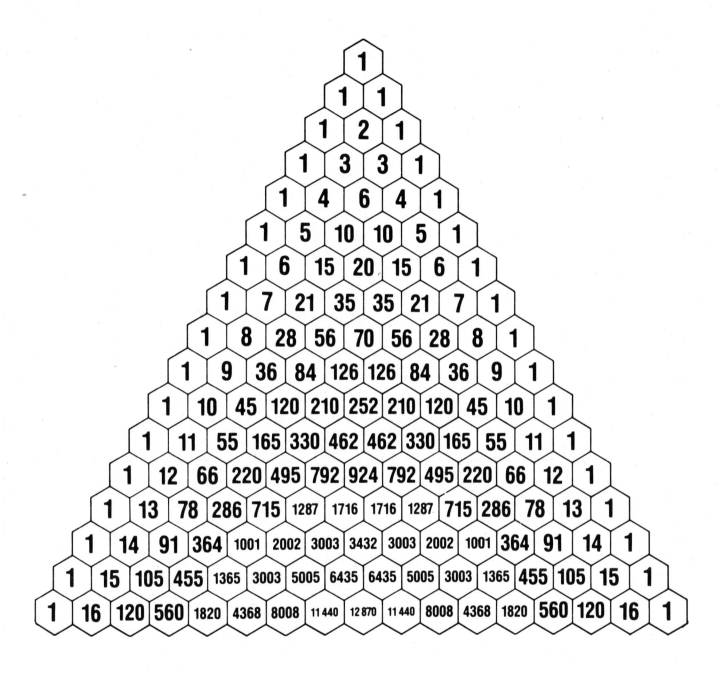

PART 2: IMAGERY

DOT DESIGNS

Copy each design.

1.

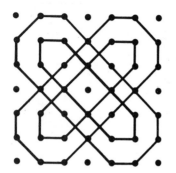

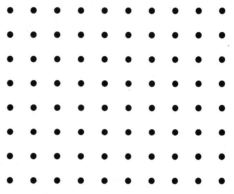

2.

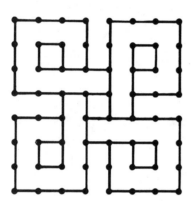

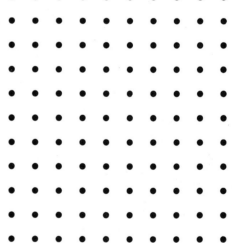

3.

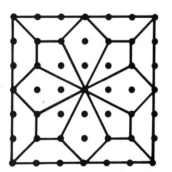

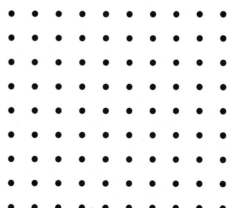

4.

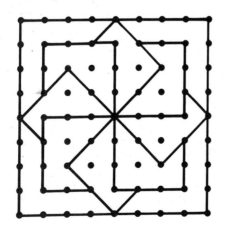

   CRITICAL THINKING ACTIVITIES IN PATTERNS, IMAGERY, LOGIC   Dale Seymour Publications

ORDER BY SIZE

1. Order the shapes from smallest (1) to largest (8).

2. Order the shapes from largest (1) to smallest (8).

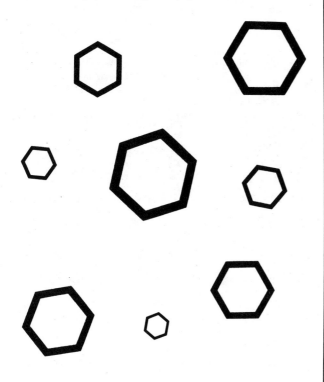

3. Order the shapes from smallest (1) to largest (10).

PERCEPTION PUZZLE

Cut apart the puzzle pieces. Put them together to make the picture.

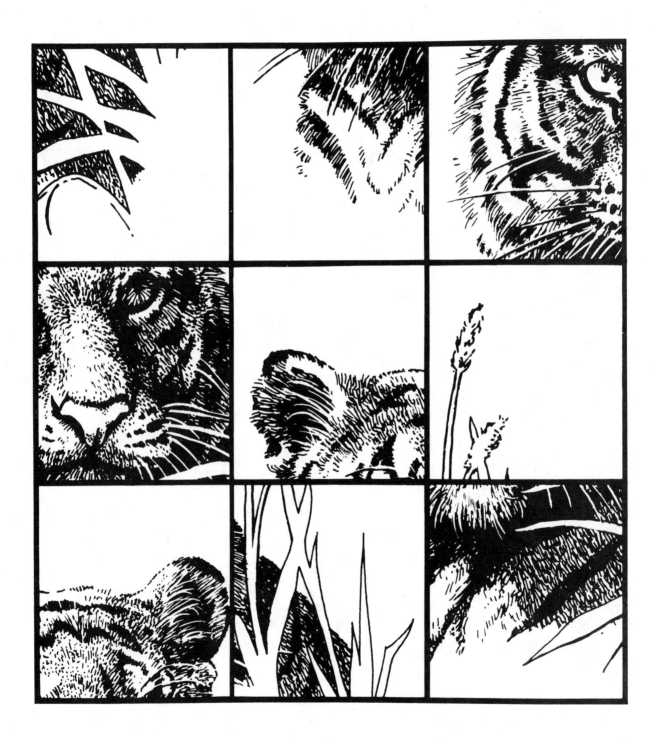

CRITICAL THINKING ACTIVITIES IN PATTERNS, IMAGERY, LOGIC   Dale Seymour Publications

COMPARING SHAPES

1. Find two pairs of designs that are alike. Write the letters for each pair.

_____   _____

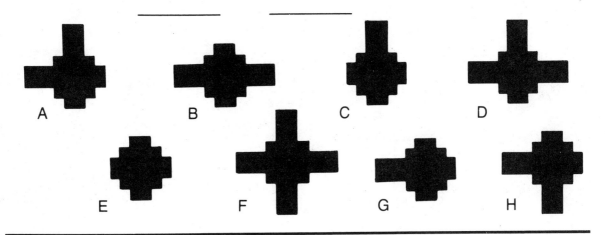

A   B   C   D

E   F   G   H

2. Which design is just like A? Draw a ring around the letter.

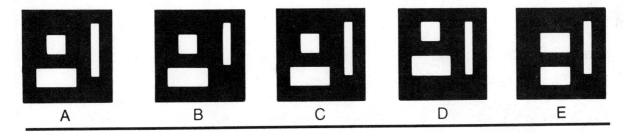

A   B   C   D   E

3. Match the pieces that are the same shape. Write the correct letter in each piece.

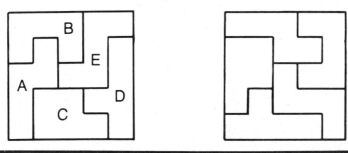

4. Match the pieces that are the same shape. Write the correct letter in each piece.

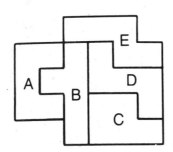

SYMMETRY SYMBOLS

Which M's are symmetrical? Draw a ring around
the letter of each one that is. Use the first M as an example.

1.

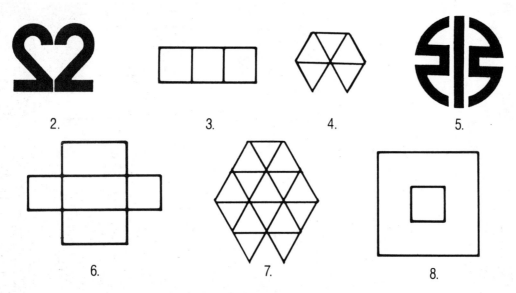

For each figure, draw the vertical line that
divides it into two symmetrical parts.

Draw the other half of each figure. Make it the same
on the right side as on the left side.

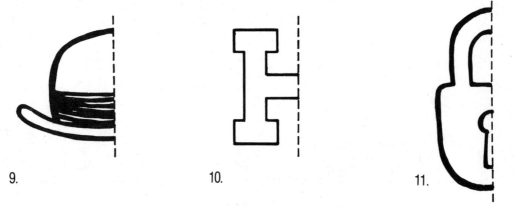

CRITICAL THINKING ACTIVITIES IN PATTERNS, IMAGERY, LOGIC   Dale Seymour Publications

MATCH AND PATCH

Match each numbered shape below with an identical lettered shape. Write the correct number in each lettered shape.

★

CUT-UPS

Which line (or lines) cuts each figure into two identical pieces?
Check your answers by cutting each figure along the line and
placing one piece on top of the other.

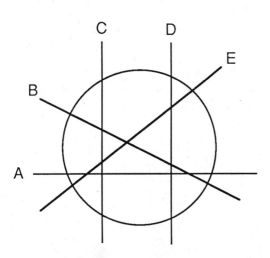

1. _____

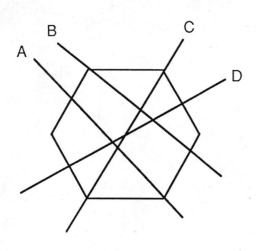

3. _____

2. _____

4. _____

PUZZLE SHAPES

1. Locate the identical shape.
   Write the letter in each shape.

2. Locate the identical shape.
   Write the letter in each shape.

3. Locate the identical shape.
   Write the letter in each shape.

MATCH THE PATCH

Match each group of shapes at left with a group at right.
Draw a square around each group that is a match. Write the number
in the center. The first one is done for you.

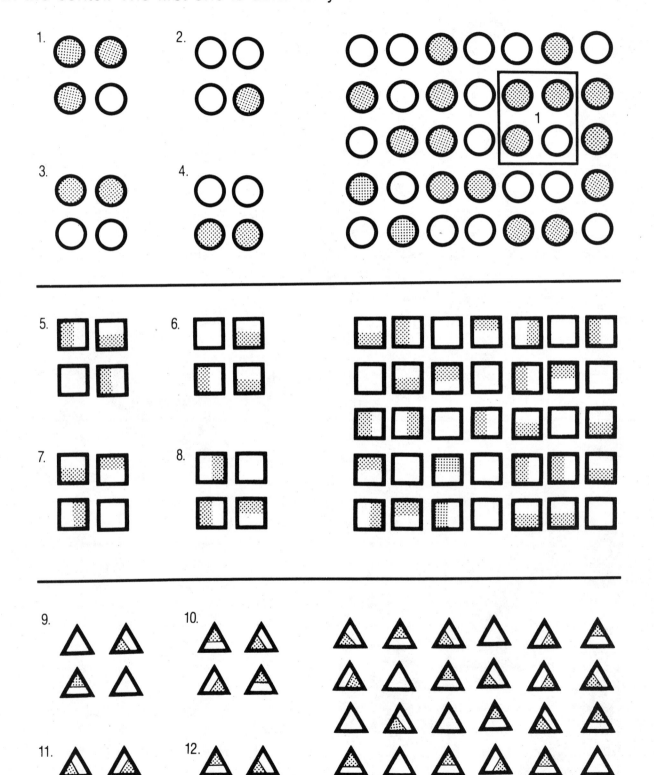

CRITICAL THINKING ACTIVITIES IN PATTERNS, IMAGERY, LOGIC   Dale Seymour Publications

CUBE PATTERNS

Each pattern below is folded into a cube. Draw a ring around the
letter of the cube (or cubes) that correctly shows each pattern.

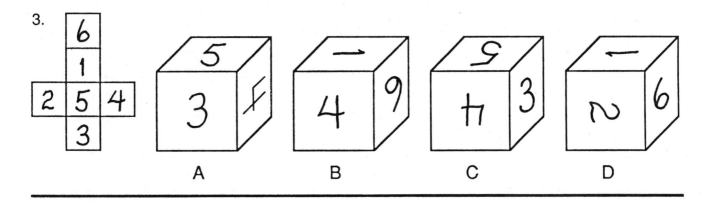

1.
```
  4
  5
3 1 2
  6
```
A   B   C   D

2.
```
  1
  6
2 4 3
  5
```
A   B   C   D

3.
```
  6
  1
2 5 4
  3
```
A   B   C   D

4.
```
  3
  6
4 5 1
  2
```
A   B   C   D

MIRROR IMAGES

Each picture below shows a sign reflected in the rearview mirror of a car.
Draw the picture that the mirror reflects. The first one is done for you.

1.

ƎJA2 ЯO�7

FOR SALE

2.

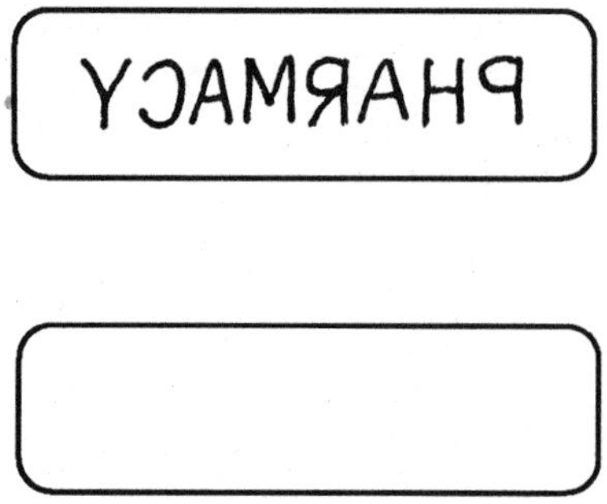

YƆAMЯAHꟼ

3.

ƎИIJO2AϽ

4.

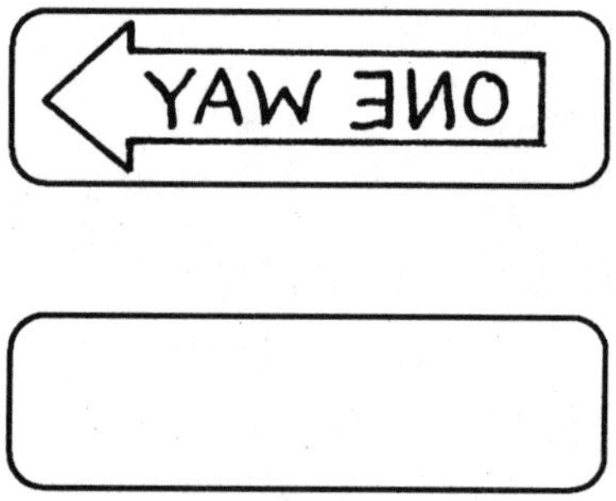

◁YAW ƎИO

5.

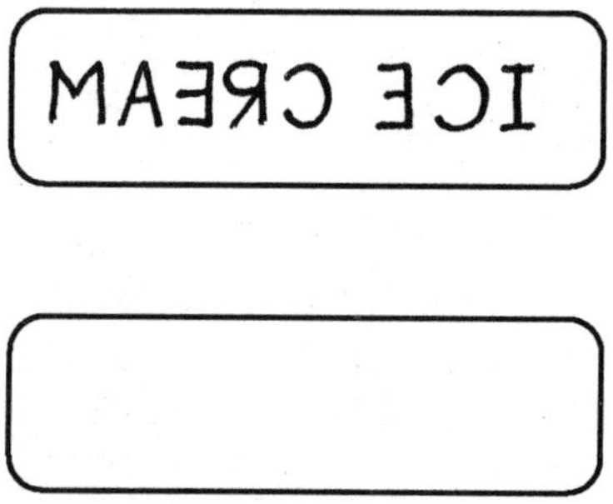

MAƎЯϽ ƎϽI

6.

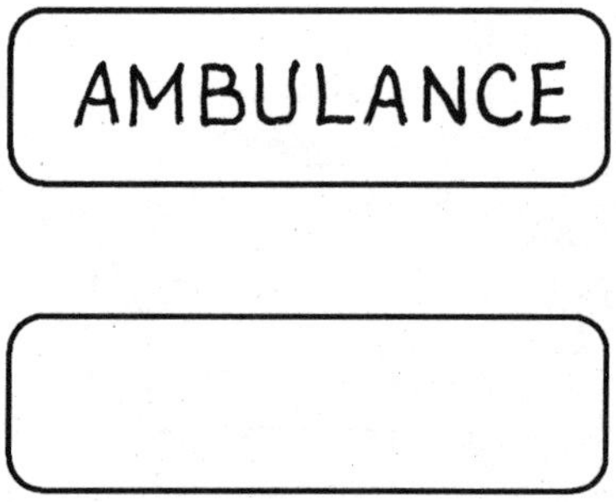

AMBULANCE

7.

UOY ꞰИAHT

8.

2ƎIVOM

CRITICAL THINKING ACTIVITIES IN PATTERNS, IMAGERY, LOGIC   Dale Seymour Publications

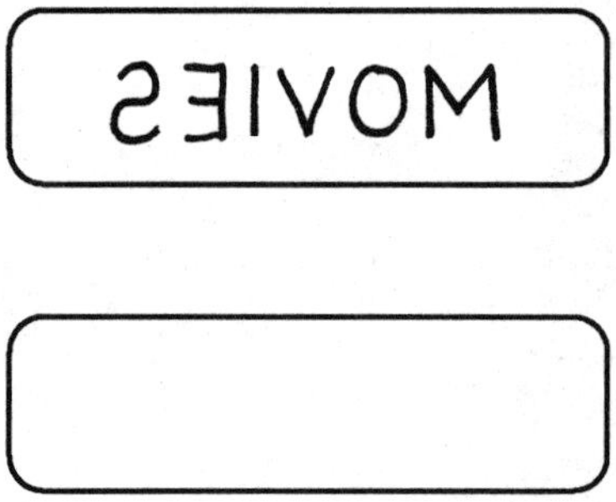

PARTS OF A WHOLE

Each drawing is in the same position in one picture in the row.
Find the picture. Ring the correct letter.

1.

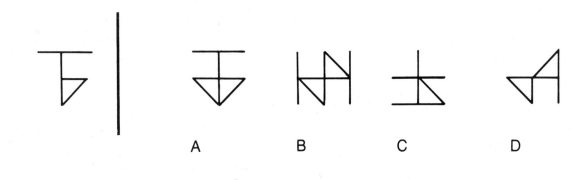

A   B   C   D

2.

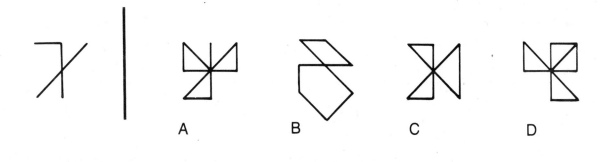

A   B   C   D

3.

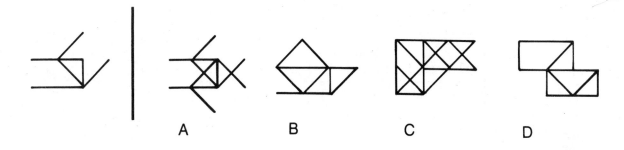

A   B   C   D

4.

A   B   C   D

CUBE PATTERNS

Draw a ring around the letter of the correct pattern for each cube.

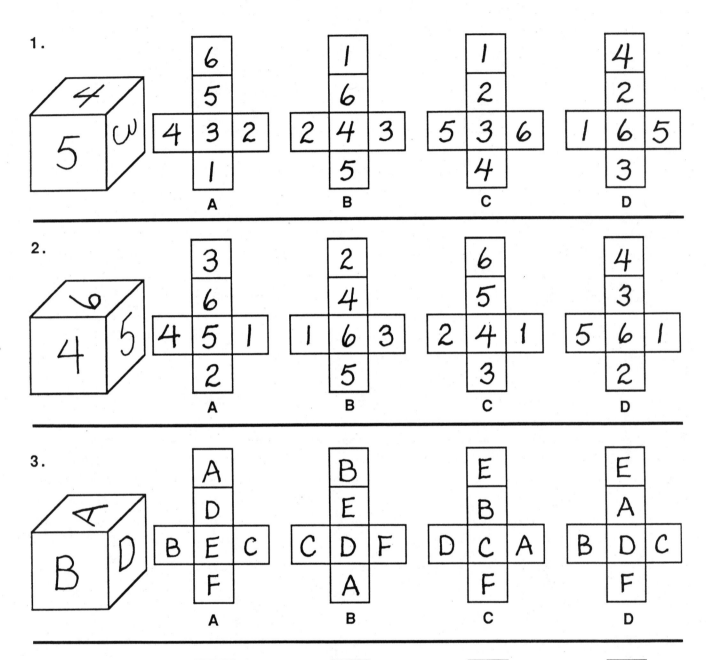

1.

A B C D

2.

A B C D

3.

A B C D

4.

A B C D

CRITICAL THINKING ACTIVITIES IN PATTERNS, IMAGERY, LOGIC   Dale Seymour Publications

DESIGNS ON DOTS

Copy each design on the blank grid below.

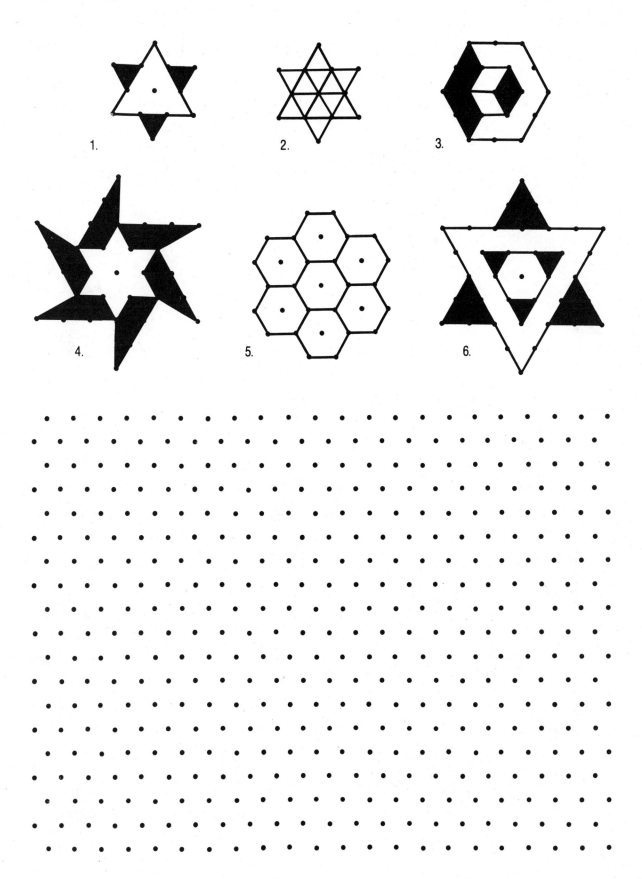

1.

2.

3.

4.

5.

6.

ORDER BY SIZE

1. Order the shapes from smallest (1) to largest (8).

2. Order the shapes from largest (1) to smallest (8).

3. Order the shapes from largest (1) to smallest (10).

CRITICAL THINKING ACTIVITIES IN PATTERNS, IMAGERY, LOGIC   Dale Seymour Publications

PICTURE PUZZLE

Can you tell what picture these puzzle pieces make? Cut out the pieces and fit them together to make the picture.

COMPARING DESIGNS

These designs are similar but not always identical. Draw a ring around the correct letter or letters.

1. Which one differs?

A   B   C   D   E

2. Which one differs?

A   B   C   D   E

3. Find two alike.

A   B   C   D   E

4. Find two alike.

A   B   C   D   E

5. Which figure is different? Two figures are still the same if they have been rotated.

A   B   C   D   E

PUZZLE SHAPES

Identify each puzzle piece below.
Write the letter in the shape.

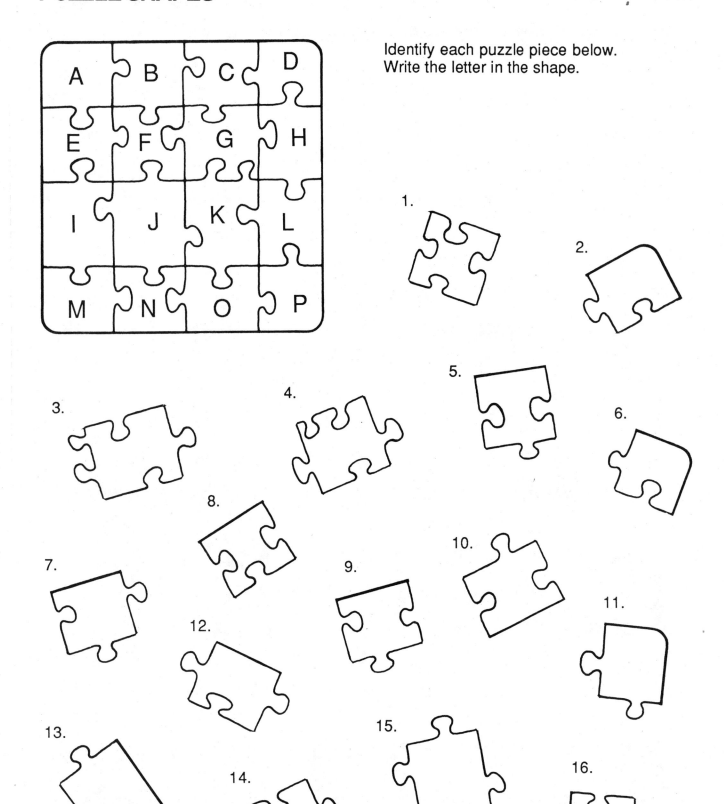

COMPARING DESIGNS

One figure is different in each series of patterns below. Draw a ring
around the letter of the figure that differs.

1.

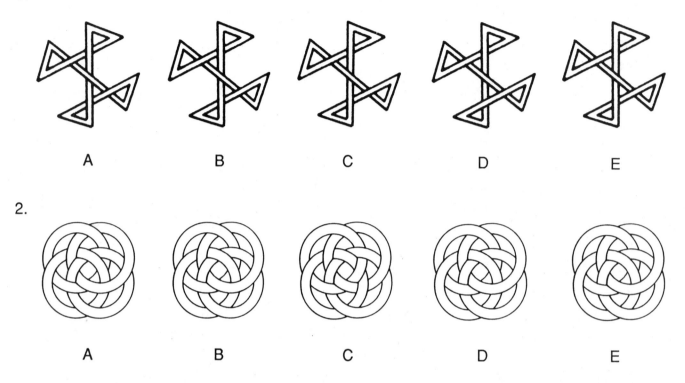

A   B   C   D   E

2.

A   B   C   D   E

3.

A   B   C   D   E

4.

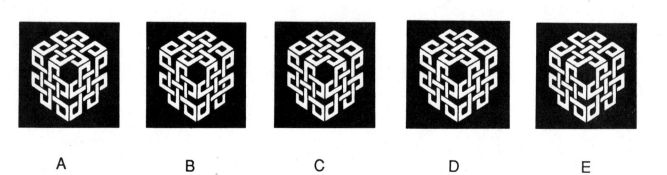

A   B   C   D   E

MIRROR IMAGES

Complete each figure. Make it symmetrical.

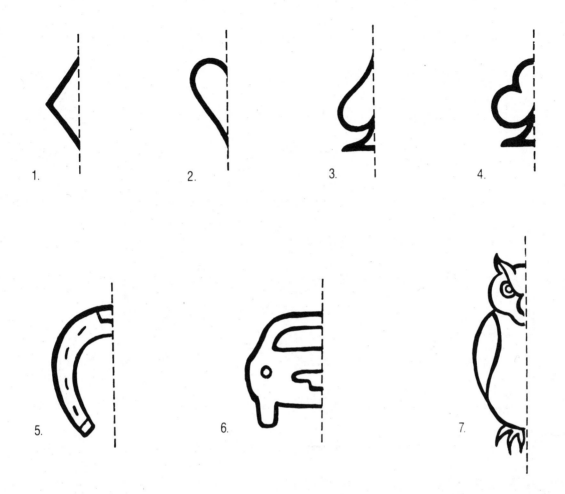

1. 2. 3. 4.

5. 6. 7.

8. Which X's have two lines of symmetry? Draw a ring around the letter of each one. Use the first X as an example.

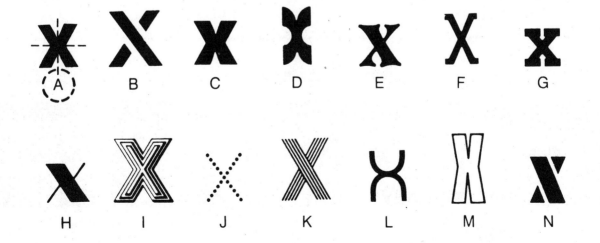

A B C D E F G

H I J K L M N

CUBE PATTERNS

Each pattern below is folded into a cube. Draw a ring around the letter of the cube (or cubes) that correctly shows each pattern.

1.

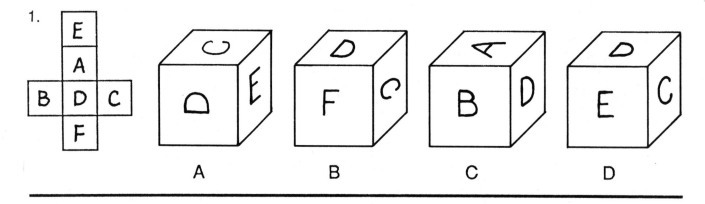

2.

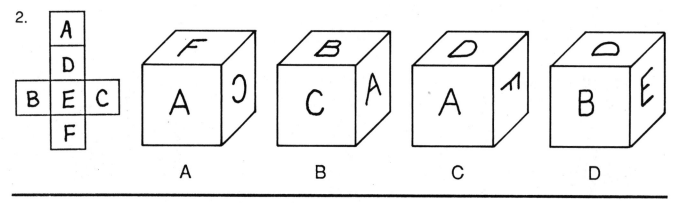

3.

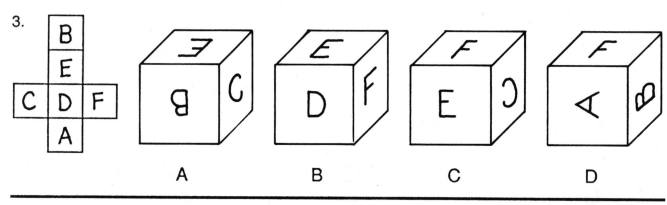

4.

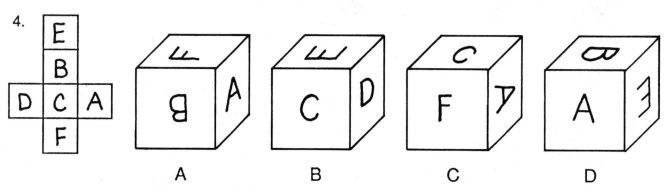

       CRITICAL THINKING ACTIVITIES IN PATTERNS, IMAGERY, LOGIC   Dale Seymour Publications

STARE AND COMPARE

1. Find the design that is exactly like A. Draw a ring around the correct letter.

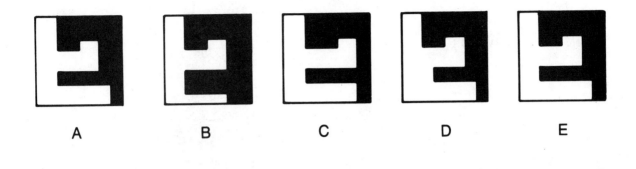

A   B   C   D   E

2. Find the piece that is exactly like A. Draw a ring around the correct letter.

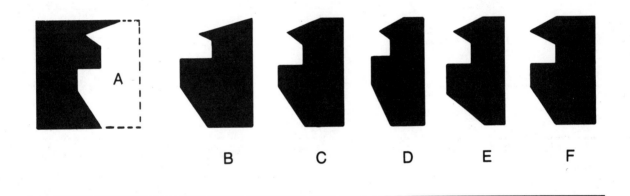

B   C   D   E   F

3. Which two pairs of shapes are exactly the same? _____ _____

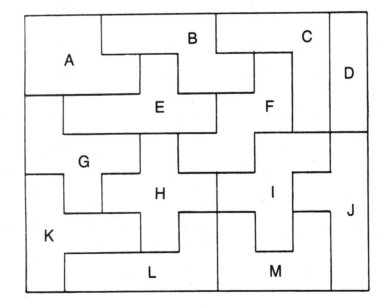

READING BACKWARDS

★★

Each of the sayings shown below is backwards or upside down.
Decode each saying and write it on the line.

1. Home, sweet home.

_____

2. Hickory, Dickory, Dock

_____

3. Look before you leap.

_____

4. To be or not to be...

_____

5. Rain, rain go away.

_____

6. A penny saved is a penny earned.

_____

7. Early to bed, early to rise.

_____

8. All's well that ends well.

_____

9. Life, liberty and the pursuit of happiness.

_____

10. Time is money.

_____

11. Who's afraid?

_____

12. A boy is man's best friend.

_____

   CRITICAL THINKING ACTIVITIES IN PATTERNS, IMAGERY, LOGIC   Dale Seymour Publications

CUBE VIEWS

Two views are shown of each cube below. Write the correct answers.

1.

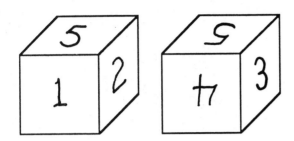

1. The cube is numbered 1, 2, 3, 4, 5, 6.

   a. Opposite the 1 is _____ .

   b. Opposite the 2 is _____ .

   c. Opposite the 5 is _____ .

2.

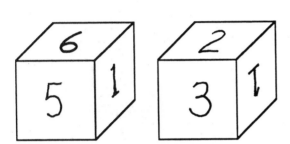

2. The cube is numbered 1, 2, 3, 4, 5, 6.

   a. Opposite the 5 is _____ .

   b. Opposite the 6 is _____ .

   c. Opposite the 1 is _____ .

3.

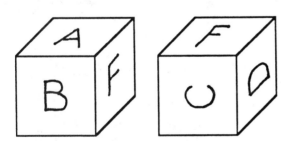

3. The cube is lettered A, B, C, D, E, F.

   a. Opposite the C is _____ .

   b. Opposite the B is _____ .

   c. Opposite the F is _____ .

4.

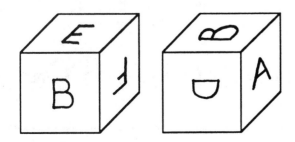

4. The cube is lettered A, B, C, D, E, F.

   a. Opposite the B is _____ .

   b. Opposite the F is _____ .

   c. Opposite the A is _____ .

PATTERN PUZZLES

Find each pattern in the square on the right. Outline each pattern using a different colored pencil. The first one is done for you. (Some patterns overlap.)

1.

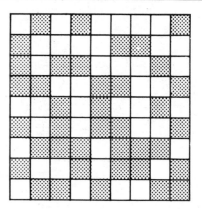

2.

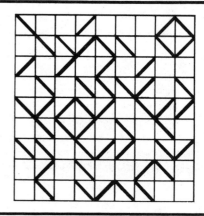

A   B   C

3.

A   B   C

4.

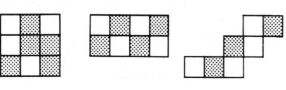

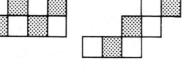

A   B   C

CRITICAL THINKING ACTIVITIES IN PATTERNS, IMAGERY, LOGIC   Dale Seymour Publications

LINES AND DESIGNS

Divide each figure in half equally in as many ways as possible.
Use the first figure as an example.

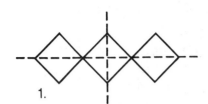

1.

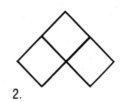

2.

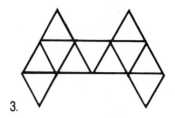

3.

4.

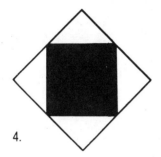

5.

6.

Copy each figure on the lines.

7.

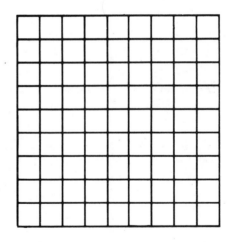

8.

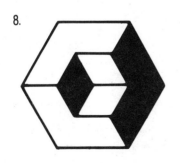

CIRCULAR REASONING

Write the letter of the correct example by each description.
There will be two extra examples.

_____ 1. three circles with the same center

_____ 2. two unequal circles with one intersecting point

_____ 3. two unequal circles with two intersecting points

_____ 4. three equal circles with six intersecting points

_____ 5. three unequal circles with one intersecting point

_____ 6. two equal circles with one intersecting point

_____ 7. three unequal circles with no intersecting points

_____ 8. four equal circles

_____ 9. three unequal circles with three intersecting points

_____ 10. seven equal circles with 13 intersecting points

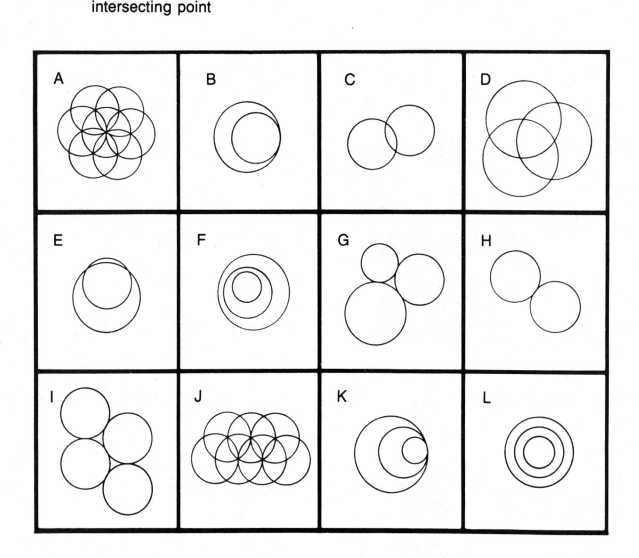

FOLDED SHAPES

Fold point A to point B. Draw a ring around the letter of the picture
that shows the result.

1.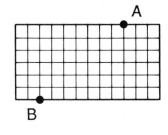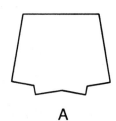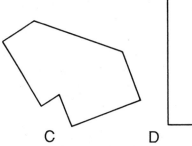

                              A   B   C   D

2.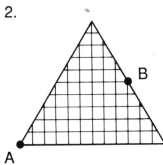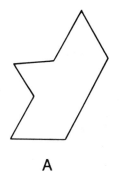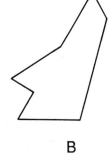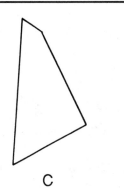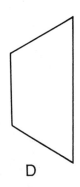

                              A   B   C   D

3.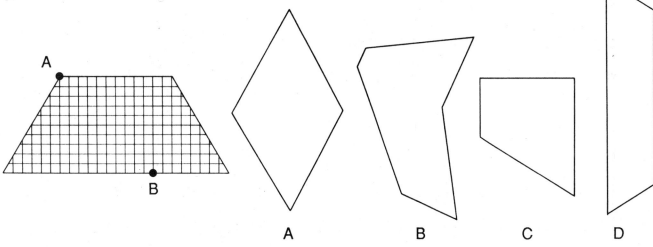

                              A   B   C   D

4.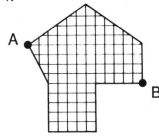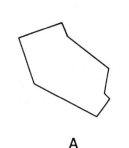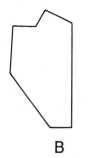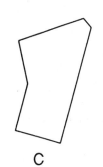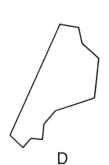

                              A   B   C   D

PICTURE PLOTTING

Follow the directions below. Draw neatly and you will have an illusion that can be seen in different ways.

1. On a sheet of $\frac{1}{4}$-inch graph paper, draw a vertical axis (reference line) about one inch in from the left edge of the paper. Draw a horizontal axis (reference line) about 2 inches up from the bottom of the page.

2. Number the squares along each axis from 1 to 20.

3. Plot (in pencil) each of the following points:
   A(2,20), B(8,20), C(14,20), D(11,17), E(17,17), F(2,14), G(8,14), H(20,14), I(5,11), J(17,11), K(2,8), L(14,8), M(20,8), N(5,5), O(11,5), P(8,2), Q(14,2), and R(20,2).

4. Accurately draw line segments $\overline{AC}$, $\overline{CH}$, $\overline{HR}$, $\overline{PR}$, $\overline{KP}$, and $\overline{AK}$. Draw them first in pencil. Then draw over the penciled lines in ink.

5. Accurately draw line segments $\overline{BD}$, $\overline{DE}$, $\overline{BG}$, $\overline{FG}$, $\overline{GL}$, $\overline{DO}$, $\overline{IJ}$, $\overline{FI}$, $\overline{EJ}$, $\overline{IN}$, $\overline{JM}$, $\overline{LM}$, $\overline{NO}$, $\overline{LQ}$, and $\overline{OQ}$. Again, draw the lines in pencil first. Then draw over the penciled lines in ink.

6. Erase all penciled letters.

7. Can you see 4 cubes in a corner? Can you see them stacked in different corners?

8. Color the drawing so it looks three-dimensional.

CRITICAL THINKING ACTIVITIES IN PATTERNS, IMAGERY, LOGIC   Dale Seymour Publications

1. Which A's have line symmetry? Draw a ring around each correct letter.

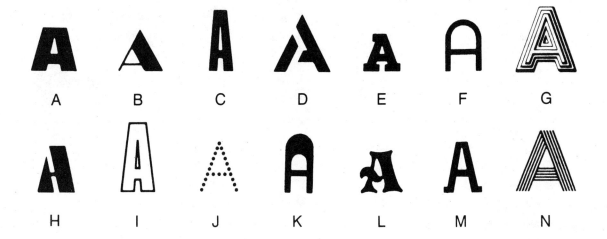

2. Which dominoes have two lines of symmetry? Draw a ring around each correct letter.

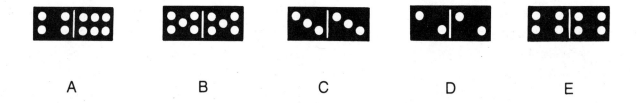

Complete each drawing to make it symmetrical.

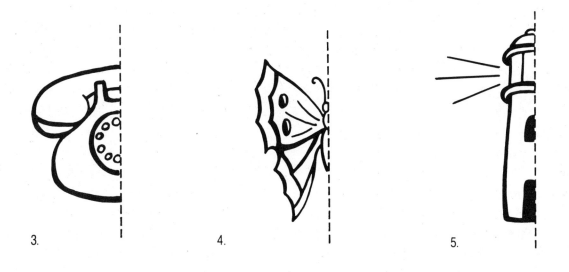

3.

4.

5.

GRID DESIGNS

Copy each design on the blank grid below.

1.

2.

3.

4.

5.

6.

PUZZLE PARTS

What picture will these puzzle pieces make? Cut apart the pieces
and fit them together to make the picture.

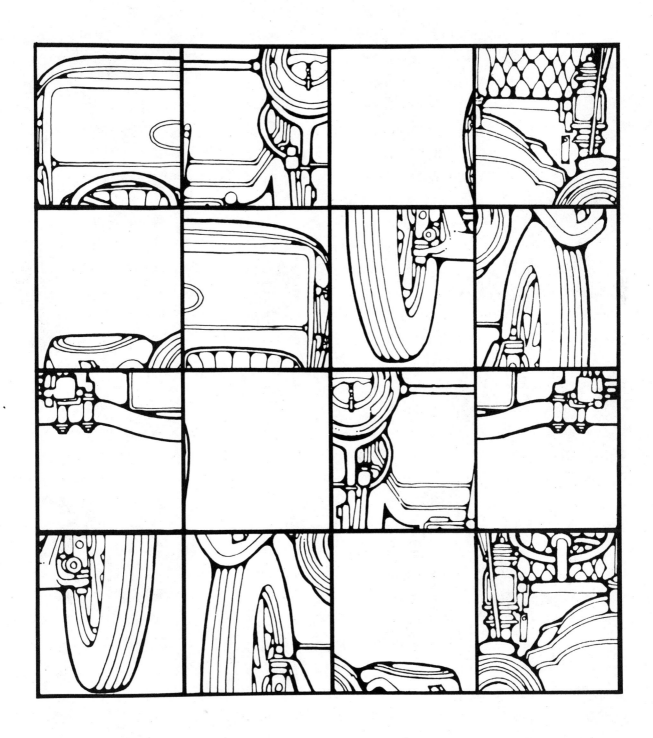

PARTS OF A WHOLE

Each shape on the left can be formed using three of the numbered pieces on the right. Write the letter of the shape next to each of its numbered pieces. Some pieces may be used to make more than one shape.

CREATIVE BISECTING

Two shapes are congruent if they have exactly the same size and shape. Divide each of the large squares below into two congruent shapes. The grid lines are provided to assist you. The first four squares are done as examples.

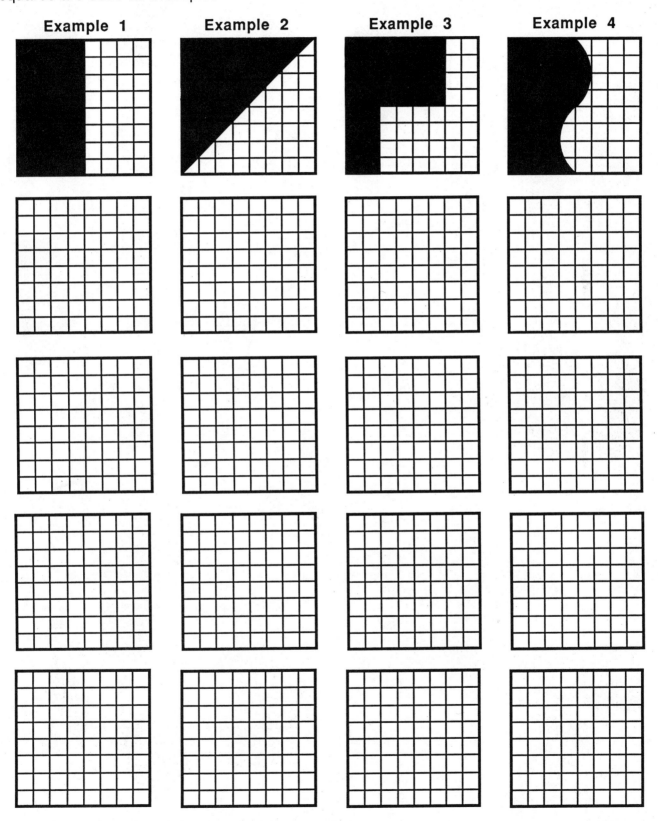

Example 1   Example 2   Example 3   Example 4

PUZZLE SHAPES

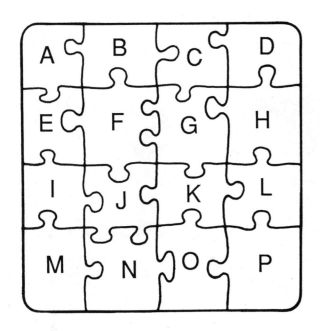

Identify each puzzle piece below.
Write the letter in the shape.

1.

2.

3.

4.

5.
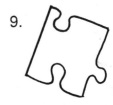

6.
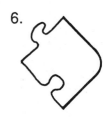

7.
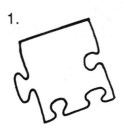

8.

9.

10.
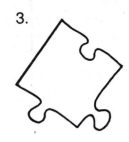

11.

12.
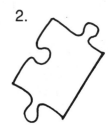

13.

14.
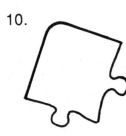

15.
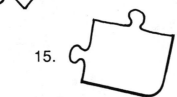

16.

CRITICAL THINKING ACTIVITIES IN PATTERNS, IMAGERY, LOGIC   Dale Seymour Publications

GRIDS AND SYMMETRY

Copy each figure on the grid.

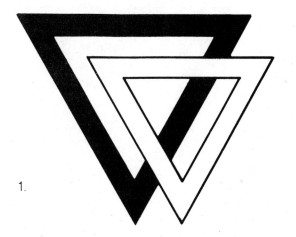

1.

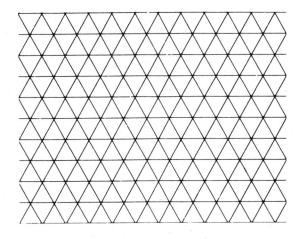

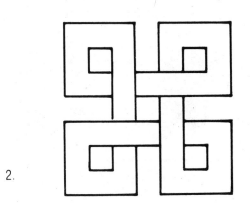

2.

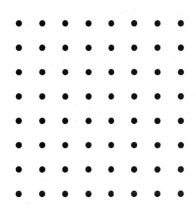

Draw all lines of symmetry on each figure. (Some figures have more than two; others have none.)

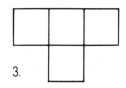

3.

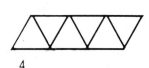

4.

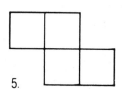

5.

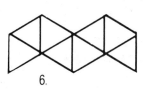

6.

7.

8.

9.

10.

CRAZY SHAPES

1. Find the design that is exactly like A. Draw a ring around the correct letter.

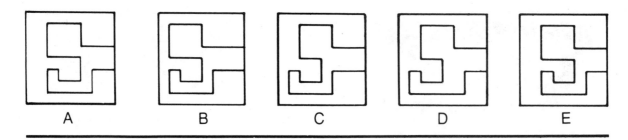

2. Find two congruent shapes. Draw a ring around each correct letter.

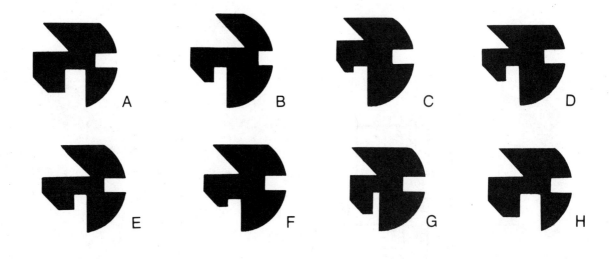

3. Write the correct letter in each congruent shape.

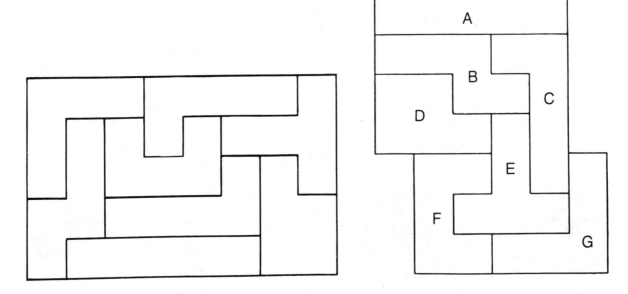

COMPARING DESIGNS

These designs are similar but not always identical. Draw a ring around the correct letter or letters.

1. Which one differs?

A   B   C   D   E

2. Which one differs?

A   B   C   D   E

3. Two of these figures are alike even though they are rotated. Which two are the same?

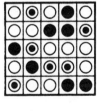   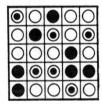   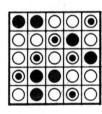   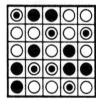   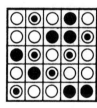

A   B   C   D   E

4. Find two alike. The figures are rotated.

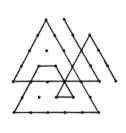      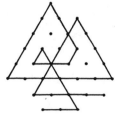      

A   B   C   D   E

FINE LINES

Trace the shape as it appears in each box in the row.

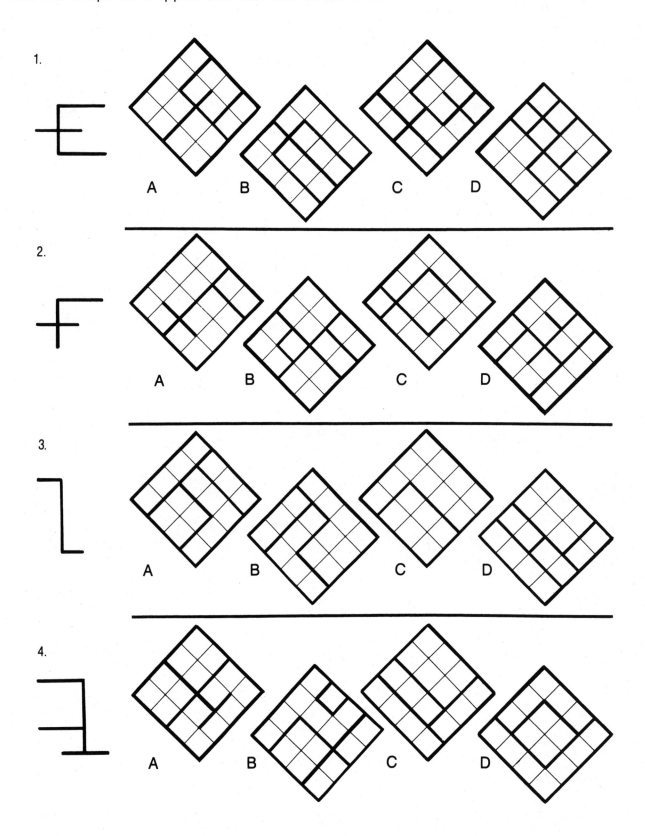

1.

A   B   C   D

2.

A   B   C   D

3.

A   B   C   D

4.

A   B   C   D

CRITICAL THINKING ACTIVITIES IN PATTERNS, IMAGERY, LOGIC   Dale Seymour Publications

MIRROR DRAWINGS

★★★

Draw each picture as it would look reflected in the rearview mirror
of a car. The first one is done as an example.

1.

2.

3.

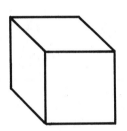

4.

5.

6.

7.

8.

READING BACKWARDS ★★★

Each of the sayings below is backwards or upside down.
Decode the saying and write it on the line.

1. Absence makes the heart grow fonder.

_____

2. Two's company, three's a crowd.

_____

3. Dr. Livingston, I presume.

_____

4. All for one, one for all.

_____

5. Little strokes fell great oaks.

_____

6. All men are created equal.

_____

7. A picture is worth a thousand words.

_____

8. Don't put all your eggs in one basket.

_____

CRITICAL THINKING ACTIVITIES IN PATTERNS, IMAGERY, LOGIC   Dale Seymour Publications

DIRECTIONAL TURNS

Which direction will each cog turn? Write your answers as
cw for clockwise, or **ccw** for counterclockwise. The direction
of movement is given for one cog in each problem below.

1.

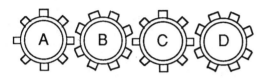

	A	B	C	D
	CW	___	___	___
	CCW	___	___	___

2.

	A	B	C	D	E
	___	___	CW	___	___
	___	___	___	CCW	___

3.

	A	B	C	D
	CW	___	___	___

4.

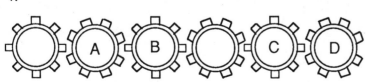

	A	B	C	D
	___	CCW	___	___

FOLDED SHAPES

Fold point A to point B. Draw a ring around the letter of the picture
that shows the result.

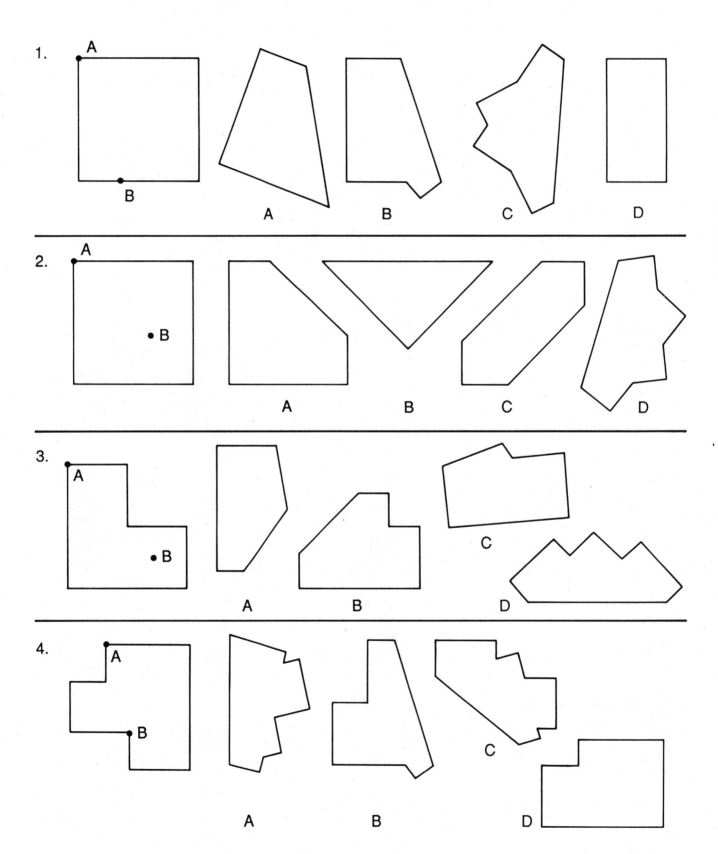

CRITICAL THINKING ACTIVITIES IN PATTERNS, IMAGERY, LOGIC   Dale Seymour Publications

PARTS OF A WHOLE

When three of the figures in each row below are placed on top of each other, the entire figure is shaded and none of the shading overlaps. Draw a ring around the three correct letters in each row.

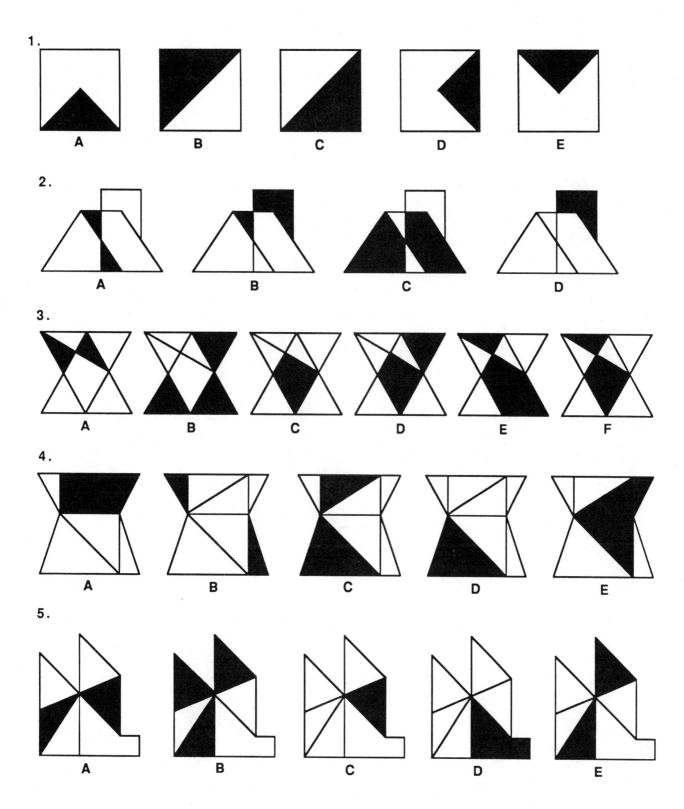

CUBE VIEWS

Two views are shown of each cube below. Write the correct answers.

1. The cube is marked ○, □, △, ⌒, 0, ⬡

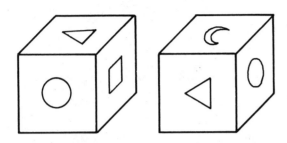

    a. Opposite the △ is _____ .

    b. Opposite the ○ is _____ .

    c. Opposite the □ is _____ .

2. The cube is marked ○, □, △, ⌒, 0, ⬡

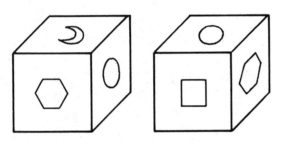

    a. Opposite the ⬡ is _____ .

    b. Opposite the □ is _____ .

    c. Opposite the ○ is _____ .

3. The cube is marked ⚀, ⚁, ⚂, ⚃, ⚄, ⚅

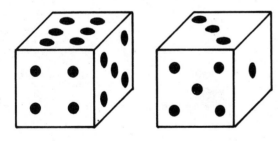

    a. Opposite the ⚁ is _____ .

    b. Opposite the ⚂ is _____ .

    c. Opposite the ⚅ is _____ .

4. The cube is marked ⚀, ⚁, ⚂, ⚃, ⚄, ⚅

 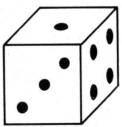

    a. Opposite the ⚃ is _____ .

    b. Opposite the ⚁ is _____ .

    c. Opposite the ⚅ is _____ .

HIDDEN SHAPES

Study the figure below to see if you can find each of the following shapes:

1. a cube
2. a cylinder
3. a square pyramid
4. a perfect 5-pointed star
5. a rectangular prism
6. a cone

Use a different color of pencil or pen to trace each shape.

CUBE PATTERNS

Each pattern below is folded into a cube. Draw a ring around the letter of the cube (or cubes) that correctly shows each pattern.

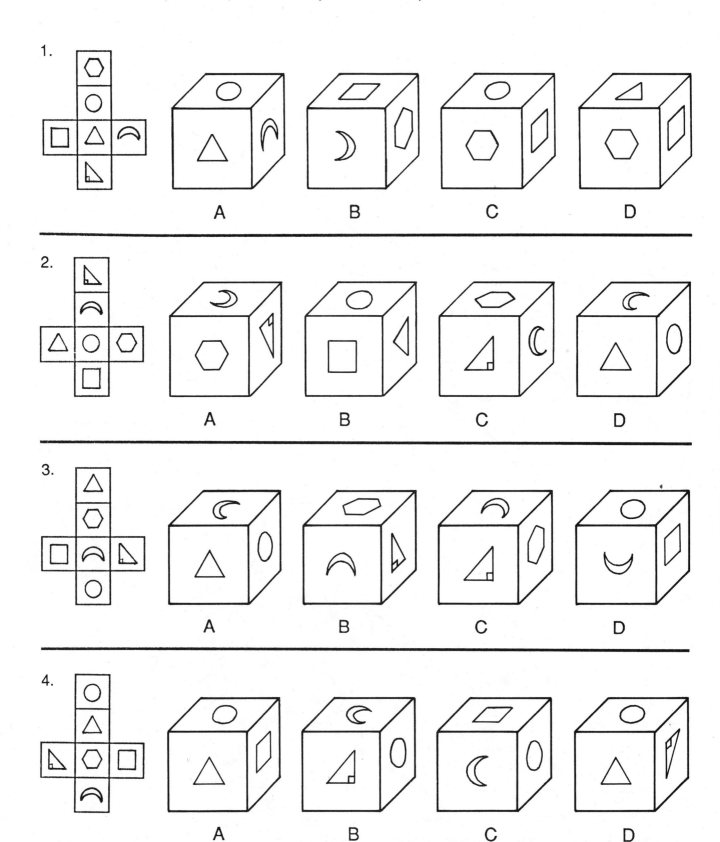

CRITICAL THINKING ACTIVITIES IN PATTERNS, IMAGERY, LOGIC   Dale Seymour Publications

POINTS AND LINES

Carefully draw each of the following. Use only a pencil.

1. All points $\frac{1}{2}$ inch from point **A**. • **A**	2. All points the same distance from **B** and **C**. • **C** **B** •	3. The shortest route from point **D** to line **e**. **e** • **D**
4. All points midway between lines **f** and **g**. **f** **g**	5. All points about $\frac{1}{8}$ inch from the square.	6. All points about $\frac{1}{8}$ inch from the figure.
7. All points about $\frac{1}{2}$ inch from segment $\overline{HI}$. **H** **I**	8. Several lines perpendicular to $\overline{JK}$. **K** **J**	9. One line perpendicular to $\overline{LM}$ at point **P**. **L** **P** **M**
10. All points the same distance from the two lines below.	11. All points about $\frac{1}{2}$ inch from line **s** or about $\frac{1}{2}$ inch from point **T**. **s** • **T**	12. All points about $\frac{1}{2}$ inch from line **s** and about $\frac{1}{2}$ inch from point **T**. **s** • **T**

ILLUSIONS

Plot this drawing on a sheet of graph paper that has 8 squares to the inch. If you follow these directions accurately, you will draw an interesting illusion.

1. Draw a vertical axis on the graph paper about one inch from the left edge. Draw a horizontal axis about one inch from the bottom.
2. Number the squares along the vertical axis by 5's from 1 to 65. Number the squares along the horizontal axis by 5's from 1 to 45.
3. Draw 3 circles, each with a $\frac{1}{2}$-inch radius. Draw them so the center of one circle is at (8,8), the center of another is at (24,8), and the center of the third is at (40,8).
4. Plot points A(4,8), B(4,56), and C(36,61).
5. Draw line segments $\overline{AB}$ and $\overline{BC}$.
6. Plot points D(36,8), E(44,56), and F(44,8).
7. Draw line segments $\overline{DC}$, $\overline{CE}$, and $\overline{EF}$.
8. Plot points G(12,8), H(12,46), and I(28,48).
9. Draw line segments $\overline{GH}$ and $\overline{HI}$.
10. Plot points J(28,8), K(28,42), L(20,41), and M(20,8).
11. Draw line segments $\overline{IJ}$, $\overline{LK}$, $\overline{HL}$, and $\overline{LM}$.
12. Color the drawing so it looks three-dimensional.

CRITICAL THINKING ACTIVITIES IN PATTERNS, IMAGERY, LOGIC   Dale Seymour Publications

PART 3: LOGIC

STRINGS ATTACHED

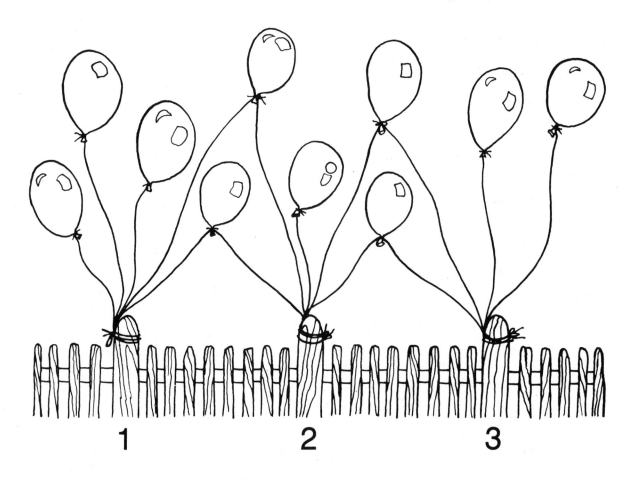

How many balloons are tied to:

1. two different posts? _____

2. both posts 1 and 2? _____

3. both posts 2 and 3? _____

4. post 1 only? _____

5. post 2 only? _____

6. post 3 only? _____

7. post 2 or post 3 only? _____

8. post 1 or post 2 only? _____

    CRITICAL THINKING ACTIVITIES IN PATTERNS, IMAGERY, LOGIC   Dale Seymour Publications

OH BROTHER!

None of the four Jones brothers is the same height.
No brother is taller than a brother who is older.
The brothers' names are Don, Dan, Dave, and Dick.

Read these three statements. Then answer the questions.
Dave is taller than Dan and Dick.
Don is older than Dave.
Dan is shorter than Dick.

1. Who is older, Dick or Dave? _____

2. Who is younger, Dave or Dan? _____

3. Which brother is older than Dan but younger than Dave? _____

4. Who is the oldest? _____

5. Who is the youngest? _____

MOO-VING LOGIC

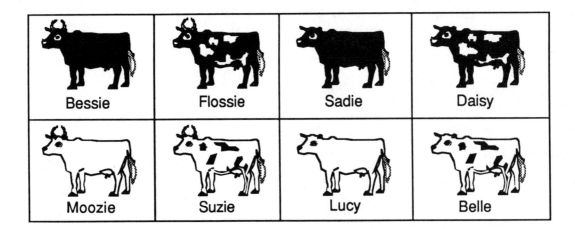

| Bessie | Flossie | Sadie | Daisy |
| Moozie | Suzie | Lucy | Belle |

1. One herd has four black cows, some with spots and some without. What are their names?

   _____

2. Another herd has four white cows, some with spots and some without. What are their names?

   _____

3. Four cows went to the fair. All had spots. What were their names?

   _____

4. Four cows usually stand under the apple tree in the pasture. All have horns. What are their names?

   _____

5. Four cows had calves in the spring. None of the cows had horns. What were their names?

   _____

6. All the cows with spots and all the cows with horns came into the barn when it rained. Name the cows that did not.

   _____

7. The black cows, the cows with spots, and the cows without horns do not wear bells. Which cow wears a bell?

   _____

8. At night, all the cows came into the barn but one. The white cows, the cows with horns, and the black cows without spots came in. Which one was missing?

   _____

9. Each of the farmer's two children had a favorite cow. Both cows had horns and spots but were different colors. What were the cows' names?

   _____

10. Seven cows went for a walk around the pasture. The black cows with horns, the white cows with horns, and the black cows with spots went. The black cows without horns and the white cows without spots also went. Name the cow that didn't go.

    _____

CRITICAL THINKING ACTIVITIES IN PATTERNS, IMAGERY, LOGIC Dale Seymour Publications

NUMBER SENSE

Draw a ring around each correct answer.

1. My number is the same as yours.
   So, your number could be greater than
   mine.   true   false

2. Our numbers are both even numbers.
   So, our numbers must be the same.   true   false

3. My number is 5 less than yours.
   So, your number is 5 greater than mine.   true   false

4. My number is greater than José's but less
   than yours.
   So, your number is greater than José's.   true   false

5. Your number is 2.
   My number is 7 greater than your number.
   So, my number is greater than 9.   true   false

6. My number ends in 5.
   Your number is 6 greater than my number.
   So, your number is an odd number.   true   false

7. My number is the same as Lois's.
   Lois has the same number as you.
   So, our numbers are the same.   true   false

LOCATING LETTERS

Use the letter grid at right. Follow the directions, and write the letter of your destination. The first one is done as an example.

A	B	C	D	E
F	G	H	I	J
K	L	M	N	O
P	Q	R	S	T
U	V	W	X	Y

1. Start at letter A.
    Go right two letters (to C).
    Go down three letters (to R).
    You end at ___R___ .

2. Start at letter A.
    Go down three letters.
    Go right three letters.
    You end at _____ .

3. Start at A.
    Go right 3.
    Go down 1.
    Go left 1.
    Go down 3.
    End at _____ .

4. Start at A.
    Go right 4.
    Go down 4.
    Go left 4.
    Go up 3.
    End at _____ .

5. Start at M.
    Up 2.
    Left 2.
    Down 4.
    Right 2.
    End at _____ .

6. Start at M.
    Down 2.
    Right 1.
    Up 4.
    Left 3.
    End at _____ .

7. Start at Y.
    Up 4.
    Left 4.
    Down 4.
    Right 3.
    Up 3.
    Left 2.
    Down 2.
    Right 1.
    Up 1.
    End at _____ .

8. Start at M.
    Down 1.
    Left 1.
    Up 2.
    Right 2.
    Down 3.
    Left 3.
    Up 4.
    Right 4.
    Down 4.
    End at _____ .

9. Start at T.
    Up 3.
    Left 2.
    Down 4.
    Right 1.
    Up 2.
    Left 3.
    Down 2.
    End at _____ .

10. Start at U.
    Up 1.
    Right 1.
    Up 1.
    Right 1.
    Up 1.
    Right 1.
    Up 1.
    Right 1.
    End at _____ .

CRITICAL THINKING ACTIVITIES IN PATTERNS, IMAGERY, LOGIC   Dale Seymour Publications

LETTER LOGIC

A and B stand for counting numbers.

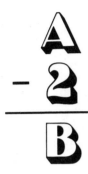

1. If A is 9, then B is _____.
2. If A is 4, then B is _____.
3. If B is 5, then A is _____.
4. If B is 10, then A is _____.
5. A – B is _____.

X, Y, and Z stand for counting numbers.

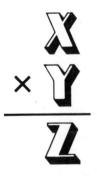

1. If X is 5 and Y is 3, then Z is _____.
2. If X is 4 and Y is 2, then Z is _____.
3. If X is 3 and Z is 12, then Y is _____.
4. If X is 2 and Z is 8, then Y is _____.
5. Name two numbers that X might be, if Z is 35.

SETS AND CIRCLES

Look at each diagram. For each set, write the letter of the best description.

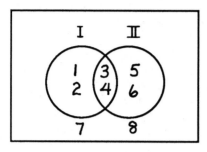

A. Numbers in Circle I
B. Numbers in Circle II
C. Numbers in both circles
D. Numbers in neither circle

1. { 1, 2, 3, 4 }   _A_

2. { 3, 4 }   _____

3. { 3, 4, 5, 6 }   _____

4. { 7, 8 }   _____

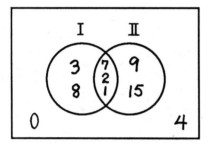

A. Numbers in Circle I
B. Numbers in Circle II
C. Numbers in both circles
D. Numbers in neither circle

5. { 1, 2, 3, 7, 8 }   _____

6. { 0, 4 }   _____

7. { 1, 2, 7 }   _____

8. { 1, 2, 7, 9, 15 }   _____

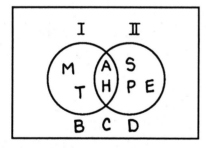

A. Letters in Circle I
B. Letters in Circle II
C. Letters in both circles
D. Letters in neither circle

9. { A, H, M, T }   _____

10. { A, H }   _____

11. { B, C, D }   _____

12. { A, E, H, P, S }   _____

    CRITICAL THINKING ACTIVITIES IN PATTERNS, IMAGERY, LOGIC   Dale Seymour Publications

COMPARING SYMBOLS

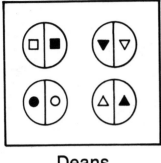

Deans

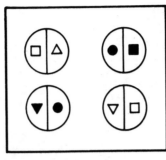

Means

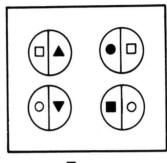

Feans

1. Which of the following is a Mean? _____

    A   B   C   D

2. Which of the following is a Fean? _____

    A   B   C   D

3. Which of the following are neither Means nor Deans? _____

    A   B   C   D

4. Draw a picture of another Dean.

STATE-A-DATE

List the dates below without looking at a calendar.

1. April 23rd falls on Saturday. List the dates of the other Saturdays in April.

   _____

2. February 14th falls on Sunday. List the dates of the Wednesdays in February.

   _____

3. August 12th falls on Wednesday. List the dates of the other Wednesdays in August.

   _____

4. January 1st falls on Friday. List the dates of the Mondays in January.

   _____

5. September 7th falls on Monday. List the dates of the Wednesdays in September.

   _____

6. May 6th falls on Friday. List the dates of the Thursdays in May.

   _____

7. November 24th falls on Thursday. List the dates of the Fridays in November.

   _____

8. March 1st falls on Monday. List the dates of the Sundays in March.

   _____

9. December 25th falls on Sunday. List the dates of the Sundays in the following January.

   _____

10. October 31st falls on Tuesday. List the dates of the other Tuesdays in October.

   _____

CRITICAL THINKING ACTIVITIES IN PATTERNS, IMAGERY, LOGIC   Dale Seymour Publications

ORDER SORTER

Begin at START. Follow the directions. Do not do the steps in numerical order. Instead, do them in the directed order until you reach STOP. Write your results.

A. START
1. Do #5.
2. Write "end" then STOP.
3. Write the word "math" then do #8.
4. Write "36 − 9 = 27" then do #6.
5. Do #3.
6. Write "happy day" then do #9.
7. Write "Math is fun." then do #4.
8. Write "6 + 8 = 14" then do #10.
9. Write "7 is a factor of 21."
10. Do #2.

_____

B. START
1. Do #10.
2. Say "I love math" aloud then do #4.
3. Do #8.
4. Write "Math is easy." 5 times then do #7.
5. Do #9.
6. Write "I hope this is over soon." then do #9.
7. Write "Smiles" then do #6.
8. Do #5.
9. Write "Is this all?" then STOP.
10. Do #3.

_____

C. START
1. Write "Mathematics" then do #8.
2. Write "of" then do #6.
3. Write "exciting," then do #5.
4. Write "the" then do #10.
5. Write "and" then do #7.
6. Write "powerful," then do #3.
7. Write "useful" then do #9.
8. Write "is" then do #4.
9. Write "ideas." then STOP.
10. Write "study" then do #2.

_____

_____

D. START
1. Write "One," then do #10.
2. Write "four," then do #6.
3. Write "Five," then do #9.
4. Write "Hear the cow moo." then do #8.
5. Write "Fiddlesticks" then do #7.
6. Write "I hope there's no more." then do #3.
7. Write a period, then STOP.
8. Write "Three," then do #2.
9. Write "six," then do #5.
10. Write "two," then do #4.

_____

_____

TABLE LOGIC

Each member of the Sanchez family always sits in the same place at dinner. The Sanchez children are Juan, Isabel, Maria, and Ramon. Use the facts below to help locate where family members sit.

Mrs. Sanchez sits opposite Mr. Sanchez.
Juan sits opposite Maria.
Ramon sits on Mr. Sanchez's right.
Maria sits on Mrs. Sanchez's left.

Answer these questions.

1. Who sits to the right of Juan? _____

2. Who sits opposite Ramon? _____

3. Who sits between Mrs. Sanchez and Ramon? _____

4. Who sits to the right of Isabel? _____

5. Who sits between Juan and Ramon? _____

6. Who sits on Maria's left? _____

7. Who sits opposite Isabel? _____

8. Who sits to the right of Maria? _____

CRITICAL THINKING ACTIVITIES IN PATTERNS, IMAGERY, LOGIC   Dale Seymour Publications

LETTER PERFECT

Each list of words below is formed from letters in a box. A new box of
letters is used for each list. Determine the least number of letters that
could be in each box, then write your list of letters. Each letter in a box
can be used more than once. The first one is done as an example.

1. CAT, DOCK, LOCK
    What letters are in the box? __CATDOKL_____

2. MADE, BENT, DANCE
    What letters are in the box? _____

3. TOURS, PRY, PROM, CRUMB
    What letters are in the box? _____

4. FACTOR, MATH, FRACTION
    What letters are in the box? _____

5. ANGLE, PLANE, LINE, TRIANGLE
    What letters are in the box? _____

6. EQUAL, SQUARE, REASON, LEAST
    What letters are in the box? _____

7. DISTANCE, GRAM, LITER
    What letters are in the box? _____

8. EQUATION, FORMULA, CUBE, OBTUSE
    What letters are in the box? _____

9. RATIOS, ACUTE, VOLUME
    What letters are in the box? _____

10. ZERO, DECIMAL, MULTIPLE
    What letters are in the box? _____

NUMBER SENTENCES

Make the number sentences true. Write 2, 4, or 5 in each circle, but use each number only once in a problem.

1. $\bigcirc - \bigcirc = 1$

2. $\bigcirc - \bigcirc = 2$

3. $\bigcirc - \bigcirc = 3$

4. $\bigcirc + \bigcirc - \bigcirc = 1$

5. $\bigcirc + \bigcirc - \bigcirc = 3$

6. $\bigcirc + \bigcirc - \bigcirc = 7$

7. $\bigcirc \times \bigcirc - \bigcirc = 3$

8. $\bigcirc \times \bigcirc - \bigcirc = 6$

9. $\bigcirc \times \bigcirc - \bigcirc = 18$

FAVORITE GAMES

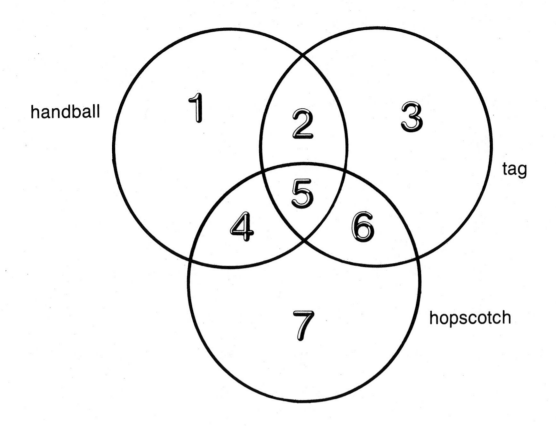

Fourth graders at Parkside School like to play
these games at recess. Where could each student
be found? Write the number of the most likely
space.

Examples: Lennie likes to play only tag. __3__

Sky is good at hopscotch but also plays handball. __4__

1. Seth's favorite game is handball. _____

2. His sister's favorite game is hopscotch. _____

3. Roxanna likes to play handball and tag but not hopscotch. _____

4. Sarina likes to play hopscotch and tag but not handball. _____

5. Gabriel plays any game. _____

EDUCATED GUESSES

A conjecture is an educated guess. Make a conjecture about each set of equations below.

1. Do these: 4 + 2 = _____   8 + 6 = _____   10 + 22 = _____
    Conjecture: The sum of two even numbers is _____ . (odd or even)

2. Do these: 7 + 9 = _____   61 + 43 = _____   25 + 3 = _____
    Conjecture: The sum of two odd numbers is _____ . (odd or even)

3. Do these: 7 + 8 = _____   14 + 19 = _____   31 + 40 = _____
    Conjecture: The sum of an odd number and an even number is _____ .
    (odd or even)

4. Do these: 12 − 6 = _____   26 − 12 = _____   64 − 36 = _____
    Conjecture: The difference of two even numbers is _____ . (odd or even)

5. Do these: 11 − 7 = _____   27 − 15 = _____   89 − 53 = _____
    Conjecture: The difference of two odd numbers is _____ . (odd or even)

6. Do these: 9 − 6 = _____   24 − 13 = _____   55 − 28 = _____
    Conjecture: The difference of an odd number and an even number is _____ .
    (odd or even)

7. Do these: 2 × 6 = _____   34 × 4 = _____   16 × 8 = _____
    Conjecture: The product of two even numbers is _____ . (odd or even)

8. Do these: 3 × 3 = _____   11 × 7 = _____   25 × 3 = _____
    Conjecture: The product of two odd numbers is _____ . (odd or even)

---

9. The sum of three even numbers
    is _____ . (odd or even)

10. The sum of three odd numbers
    is _____ . (odd or even)

11. The sum of two odd numbers and
    one even number is _____ .
    (odd or even)

12. The sum of two even numbers and
    one odd number is _____ .
    (odd or even)

13. The product of three even numbers
    is _____ . (odd or even)

14. The product of three odd numbers
    is _____ . (odd or even)

CRITICAL THINKING ACTIVITIES IN PATTERNS, IMAGERY, LOGIC   Dale Seymour Publications

LETTER LOGIC

A and B stand for counting numbers.

1. If A is 5, then B is _____.
2. If A is 4, then B is _____.
3. If B is 9, then A is _____.
4. If B is 2 times A, then A is _____.

X, Y, and Z stand for counting numbers.

1. If X is 1 and Y is 3, then Z is _____.
2. If Y is 3 and X is 4, then Z is _____.
3. If Z is 8 and Y is 1, then X is _____.
4. If Z is 9 and X is 3, then Y is _____.
5. If Z is 7, then X + Y is _____.

SHIFTING DIGITS

Follow the directions below, and write your numbers in the boxes.
The first one is done as an example.

1. Use 9, 2, 6, and 8 to get the smallest positive difference.

$$9\ 2$$
$$-\ 8\ 6$$

2. Use 3, 6, 4, 1, and 5 to get the largest positive difference.

$$\square\ \square\ \square$$
$$-\ \square\ \square$$

3. Use 3, 6, 4, 1, and 5 to get the smallest positive difference.

$$\square\ \square\ \square$$
$$-\ \square\ \square$$

4. Use 3, 6, 8, 1, 4, and 2 to get the largest positive difference.

$$\square\ \square\ \square$$
$$-\ \square\ \square\ \square$$

5. Use 3, 6, 8, 1, 4, and 2 to get the smallest positive difference.

$$\square\ \square\ \square$$
$$-\ \square\ \square\ \square$$

6. Use 3, 6, and 5 to get the smallest product.

$$\square\ \square$$
$$\times\ \square$$

7. Use 3, 6, and 5 to get the largest product.

$$\square\ \square$$
$$\times\ \square$$

8. Use 2, 1, 3, and 8 to get the largest product.

$$\square\ \square$$
$$\times\ \square\ \square$$

   CRITICAL THINKING ACTIVITIES IN PATTERNS, IMAGERY, LOGIC   Dale Seymour Publications

FINDING FIGURES

Complete the chart.

	Number
Hexagon and pentagons in all	
Squares inside circles	
Circles inside squares	
Triangles inside the octagon	
Circles not inside circles	
Polygons in all	
Polygons not inside circles	
Polygons inside circles	

FINDING NUMBERS

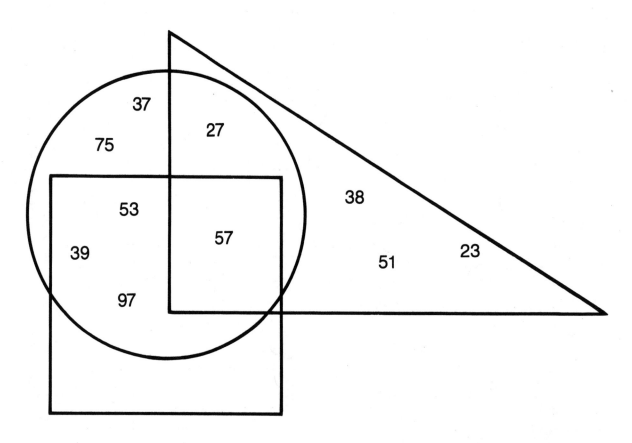

Examples: Which numbers are in both the triangle and the circle? __27, 57__

Which numbers are in the triangle but not in the circle? __23, 38, 51__

1. Which number is in all three shapes? _____

2. Which prime number is in the circle but not in the square? _____

3. Which multiples of 3 are in the triangle? _____

4. Which multiple of 3 is in the triangle and the square? _____

5. Which prime numbers are in both the circle and the square? _____

6. Which composite number is in neither the square nor the triangle? _____

7. Which composite number is in the triangle and circle but not in the square?

_____

8. Which composite number is in the square but not in the triangle? _____

FIVE-IN-A-ROW

Two people play the game of 5-in-a-row. Taking turns, one marks X's, the other marks O's. The first player to mark 5 in a row across, down, or diagonally wins. Answer the questions under each game. Identify the squares by column letters and row numbers.

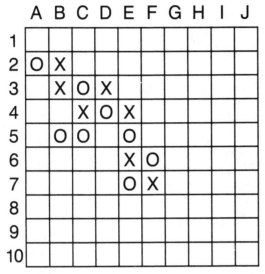

1. It's player X's turn next. Where should player X mark? _____

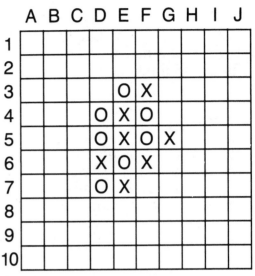

2. The player marking O's is next. Where should this player mark?

_____ or _____

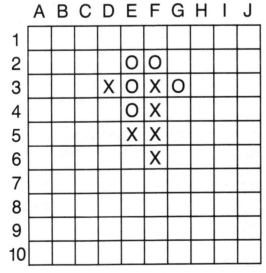

3. Whose turn is next, X's or O's?

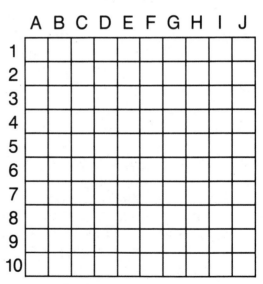

Use this grid to play 5-in-a-row with a friend.

HOW TO SOLVE IT

Use clue words such as *more, how many,* and *each* to decide how you would solve the following exercises. Do *not* solve the problems, but write how you would solve them. Use one or more of these steps:

- Choose the smaller number
- Choose the larger number
- Add the numbers
- Subtract the numbers
- Multiply the numbers
- Divide the numbers

1. Six pigs lived on the farm. Four baby pigs were born, but the farmer gave one to a neighbor. How many pigs are on the farm now?

_____

2. Eight girls and five boys went to a party. Were there more girls or more boys at the party?

_____

3. Each cow has four legs, and five cows are in the barn. Two cows leave the barn. How many cow legs are left in the barn?

_____

4. Jane has seven pennies and her brother has four pennies. Who has fewer pennies?

_____

5. Ann has three nickels. Her mother gives her six more nickels. Then Ann loses two nickels. How many nickels does she have left?

_____

6. Juan has sixteen pet slugs. José has seven pet slugs. How many more slugs does Juan have?

_____

7. Twenty apples are to be distributed equally to five people. How many apples does each person get?

_____

8. Six children are in a family. Each child has two ears and two eyes. How many ears and eyes do they have in all?

_____

9. Fifteen children came to a party. Six children stayed at the party. The children who left early were taken home in three cars. If the same number of children were in each car, how many children were in the first car?

_____

10. Kelly had 35 pennies. After recess she had only 25 pennies left. Kelly shared the pennies she gave away equally with five friends. How many pennies did each of Kelly's friends receive?

_____

CRITICAL THINKING ACTIVITIES IN PATTERNS, IMAGERY, LOGIC   Dale Seymour Publications

LETTER LOGIC

A, B, and C each stand for a different number from 1 to 9.

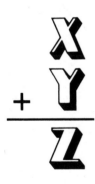

$$\begin{array}{r} A \\ + B \\ \hline C \end{array}$$

1. If all three numbers are even, what two numbers could C be? _____ or _____.

2. If B is 5 greater than A, what numbers could C be? _____ _____

3. If A is 3 times B, then C is _____ or _____.

4. If C is 6 times B, then A is _____.

5. If B is odd and A is 4 more than B, then C is _____.

6. If C is 6 more than A, then B is _____.

X, Y, and Z each stand for a different number from 1 to 9.

$$\begin{array}{r} X \\ + Y \\ \hline Z \end{array}$$

1. What is the greatest number Z could be? _____

   Why? _____

2. What is the greatest number X could be? _____

   Why? _____

   _____

3. What is the smallest number Z could be? _____

   Why? _____

   _____

4. What is the smallest number Y could be? _____

   Why? _____

   _____

   _____

CODE FEAT

A. Start with 27.	G. Divide by 3.	M. Subtract 6.
B. Start with 36.	H. Divide by 4.	N. Add 9.
C. Start with 48.	I. Divide by 6.	O. Multiply by 5.
D. Start with 54.	J. Multiply by 2.	P. Subtract 4.
E. Start with 12.	K. Multiply by 3.	Q. Add 4.
F. Start with 56.	L. Add 5.	R. Subtract 1.

In each exercise below, follow the letter sequence. Write the final answer.

Example: A   G   J   M
             27   ÷ 3 = 9   9 × 2 = 18   18 − 6 = __12__

ANSWER

1.	A	G	L	R	_____
2.	B	H	N	I	_____
3.	C	M	I	M	_____
4.	D	M	M	M	_____
5.	E	N	G	R	_____
6.	F	H	P	M	_____
7.	A	M	R	H	_____
8.	B	M	G	O	_____
9.	C	G	Q	L	_____
10.	D	I	K	M	_____
11.	E	H	O	N	_____
12.	F	R	R	I	_____
13.	C	I	J	N	_____
14.	D	G	G	K	_____
15.	E	I	K	R	_____

CRITICAL THINKING ACTIVITIES IN PATTERNS, IMAGERY, LOGIC   Dale Seymour Publications

FAVORITE SUBJECT

The four children in the Smith family each have a different favorite subject in school. Use the information given below to find out which subject each person likes best. Complete the chart. Mark an X in a square when it cannot be the answer. Mark an O to show the favorite subject.

1. Math is not Bill's favorite subject.
2. Sue doesn't like to read.
3. Sally likes art better than writing.
4. Bob's favorite subject is math.
5. Sally likes reading better than art.
6. Bill prefers writing to art.

Student	Reading	Art	Math	Writing
Bill				
Sally				
Bob				
Sue				

OUTSIDE IN

1. What numbers are:

   a. outside the smallest circle? _____

   b. inside the largest circle? _____

   c. inside two circles? _____

   d. outside exactly two circles? _____

   e. not outside any circle? _____

2. What number is:

   a. inside only the largest circle? _____

   b. inside all three circles? _____

   c. not inside any circle? _____

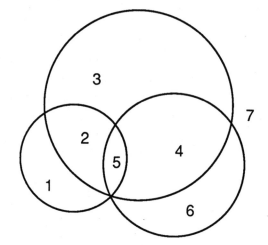

3. What letters are:

   a. outside the shaded square? _____

   b. inside the largest square? _____

   c. not outside any square? _____

   d. not inside two squares? _____

4. What letter is:

   a. outside all three squares? _____

   b. inside three squares? _____

   c. not inside the largest square nor
      outside the other two squares? _____

DESIGN CODES

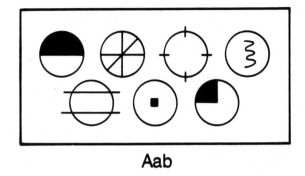

Aab

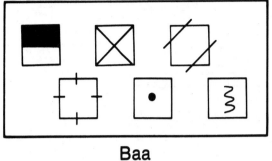

Baa

Which of the following are Baa? Draw a ring around the correct letters.

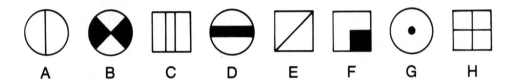

A   B   C   D   E   F   G   H

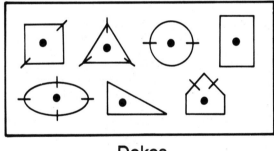

Dokos

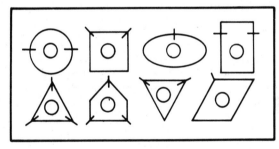

Kodos

Which of the following are Dokos? Draw a ring around the correct letters.

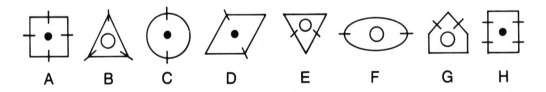

A   B   C   D   E   F   G   H

OVER HERD

Bessie	Flossie	Sadie	Daisy
Moozie	Suzie	Lucy	Belle

Can you name each cow?

1. One cow was missing at feeding time. It was black and did not have spots or horns. Which cow was missing?

   _____

2. The first cow to get to the water trough was white with spots and horns. Which cow was first?

   _____

3. One sick cow was visited by the vet. Its white spotless coat seemed pink with fever. Even its horns were drooping. Which cow was ill?

   _____

4. The cow that was usually first to be milked was black, with spots and without horns. Which cow was it?

   _____

5. The cow that was usually last to be milked was black, with horns and without spots. Which cow was it?

   _____

6. One cow won a blue ribbon at the county fair. It was white and had spots but no horns. Which cow won the blue ribbon?

   _____

7. The white cow with spots and horns wears a bell around its neck. Which cow is it?

   _____

8. Two cows were strolling in the barnyard. One was black, with spots and horns. The other was white, without spots or horns. What were their names?

   _____

9. Two cows won red ribbons at the county fair. One cow was black, with horns and without spots. The other cow was black, with spots and without horns. Which cows won red ribbons?

   _____

CRITICAL THINKING ACTIVITIES IN PATTERNS, IMAGERY, LOGIC   Dale Seymour Publications

NUMBER SENTENCES

Use each number disk only once to make the following number sentences true. Use all the disks.

1.

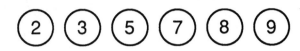

( ) + ( ) = ( )

( ) − ( ) = ( )

2.

(1)(2)(3)(4)(5)(6)(7)(8)(15)

( ) + ( ) = ( )

( ) − ( ) = ( )

( ) × ( ) = ( )

3.

(2)(3)(7)(8)(9)(10)(11)(16)(20)

( ) + ( ) = ( )

( ) − ( ) = ( )

( ) × ( ) = ( )

4.

(4)(6)(7)(8)(9)(11)(15)(24)(36)(42)(60)(72)

( ) + ( ) = ( )

( ) − ( ) = ( )

( ) × ( ) = ( )

( ) ÷ ( ) = ( )

NUMBER SENSE

Draw a ring around each correct answer.

1. My number is odd.
   Therefore, my number could be ten.   true   false

2. My number is 4.
   Your number is less than 7.
   Therefore, your number could be
   the same as mine.   true   false

3. My number is 2 greater than yours.
   Your number is even.
   Therefore, my number is odd.   true   false

4. My number is even.
   Your number is odd.
   Therefore, my number couldn't be 5.   true   false

5. My number is 5 greater than yours.
   Your number is 8.
   Therefore, my number
   is greater than 8.   true   false

6. Your number is even.
   My number is a multiple of 5.
   Therefore, our numbers
   could be the same.   true   false

7. My number is the same as Jill's.
   Jill's number is greater than Jane's.
   Therefore, Jane's number
   is less than my number.   true   false

CRITICAL THINKING ACTIVITIES IN PATTERNS, IMAGERY, LOGIC   Dale Seymour Publications

RHYME TYME

Complete these math rhymes.

1. This number is even and is less than four.
   Yes, the number is _____ , need I say more?

2. Let's find the product, do not be shy.
   To find the product, you _____ .

3. There's a branch of math that is fun to see.
   You work with figures and space—it's _____ .

4. If you have parts per hundred, do you know what is meant?
   You can do interest problems—the answer is _____ .

5. If you use a liter, gram, or meter stick,
   Then the measurement system you use is _____ .

6. If you use dividend and quotient as your guide,
   Then the operation you choose is to _____ .

7. Are numbers composite all the time?
   No, there are some special numbers that are _____ .

8. I'm thinking of a shape that I can mangle.
   It's not a square; it's a _____ .

9. In story problems some clue words "to add" will come.
   Like *how many, total,* and _____ .

10. To solve story problems you need a plan of attack.
    When told to take the difference or minus, you _____ .

DIGIT DOINGS

Find the digits that will **replace** *x* and *y* **to make the problem correct.**

1.
```
    46
    xy
  + 23
  -----
   105
```
x = _____

y = _____

2.
```
    5x
    18
  + y4
  -----
   147
```
x = _____

y = _____

3.
```
   2x3
  - 8y
  -----
   205
```
x = _____

y = _____

4.
```
    12
    1y
    x3
  + 15
  -----
    66
```
x = _____

y = _____

5.
```
    yx
  ×  6
  -----
   138
```
x = _____

y = _____

6.
```
        17y
     _____
   3) 5x9
        3
      -----
       2x
       21
      -----
        9
        9
      -----
```
x = _____

y = _____

7.
```
    4x
  × y
  -----
   315
```
x = _____

y = _____

LETTER PERFECT

The contents of two boxes are described in each problem below.
Draw a ring around T for True or F for False.

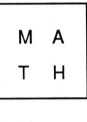

Box 1 contains the letters in the word MATH.

Box 2 contains the letters in the word FRACTION.

T	F	1.	Box 1 contains an A.
T	F	2.	Box 2 contains three vowels.
T	F	3.	Box 1 contains the letters to form the word HAM.
T	F	4.	Both boxes contain the letters to form the word HAT.
T	F	5.	Box 1 has more letters than Box 2.

Box 1 contains the letters in the word PRODUCT.

Box 2 contains the letters in the word FACTOR.

T	F	6.	Box 1 contains six letters.
T	F	7.	At least three letters are the same in both boxes.
T	F	8.	At most, four letters are the same in both boxes.
T	F	9.	The letters FA are in Box 2 but not in Box 1.
T	F	10.	The three letters in Box 1 but not in Box 2 are POD.
T	F	11.	Both boxes contain letters to form the word COT.
T	F	12.	The letter E is in neither box.
T	F	13.	The boxes contain a total of eleven different letters.

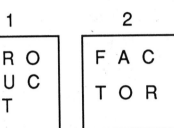

Box 1 contains the digits in the number 2,105,673.

Box 2 contains the digits in the number 987,123.

T	F	14.	Box 1 contains seven digits.
T	F	15.	Box 2 contains six digits.
T	F	16.	Exactly three digits are the same in both boxes.
T	F	17.	The sum of the common digits (digits in both boxes) is 13.
T	F	18.	The largest number formed by the digits in Box 1 that are not in Box 2 is less than 1000.
T	F	19.	The smallest number formed by the digits in Box 2 that are not in Box 1 is less than 50.
T	F	20.	Box 1 contains more odd digits than Box 2.

NUMBER SHUFFLE

Make the number sentences true. Write 2, 3, or 6 in each circle, but use each number only once in a problem.

1. $\bigcirc + \bigcirc + \bigcirc = 11$

2. $\bigcirc + \bigcirc - \bigcirc = 7$

3. $\bigcirc + \bigcirc - \bigcirc = 5$

4. $\bigcirc \times \bigcirc + \bigcirc = 20$

5. $\bigcirc \times \bigcirc + \bigcirc = 15$

6. $\bigcirc \times \bigcirc + \bigcirc = 12$

7. $\bigcirc \times \bigcirc - \bigcirc = 16$

8. $\bigcirc \times \bigcirc - \bigcirc = 9$

9. $\bigcirc \times \bigcirc - \bigcirc = 0$

10. $\bigcirc \times \bigcirc \div \bigcirc = 9$

    CRITICAL THINKING ACTIVITIES IN PATTERNS, IMAGERY, LOGIC   Dale Seymour Publications

LETTER LOGIC

A, B, C, and D each stand for a different number from 1 to 9.

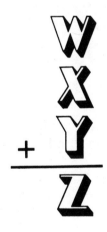

1. What number does C have to be? _____

2. If D is 6, then A is either _____ or _____.

3. If D is 7, then A is either _____ or _____.

4. If A is 4 and D is 2, then B is _____.

5. Why can't D be 1? _____

_____

_____

6. If A is 6 greater than B, then D is _____.

W, X, Y, and Z each stand for a different number from 1 to 9.

1. If W is 2, X is 3, and Y is 4, then Z is _____.

2. If W is 1, X is 2, and Z is 7, then Y is _____.

3. If W is one greater than X, Y is 1, and Z is 8, then W is _____.

4. If X is two greater than W and two less than Y, then Z has to be _____.

5. What is the smallest number Z can be? _____ Why? _____

_____

_____

ORDER SORTER

The steps needed to solve each exercise are given, but they are not in the correct order. Number them to show the correct order.

1.   643
    − 280   **Correct Order**

a. Change the 6 to 5 and write a 1 to the left of the 4. _____

b. Write the 6 below the line in the tens column. _____

c. Write a 3 below the line in the ones column. _____

d. Subtract 2 from 5. _____

e. Subtract 0 from 3. _____

f. Subtract 8 from 14. _____

g. Write a 3 below the line in the hundreds column. _____

2.   56
    + 47   **Correct Order**

a. Write the 1 in 13 above the 5. _____

b. Write the 0 in 10 below the line in the tens column. _____

c. Add 6 + 7. _____

d. Write a 1 below the line in the hundreds column. _____

e. Write the 3 in 13 below the line in the ones column. _____

f. Add 1 + 5 + 4. _____

3.   397
    + 841

a. Add 9 + 4. _____

b. Write an 8 below the line in the ones column. _____

c. Add 1 + 3 + 8. _____

d. Write the 2 in 12 below the line in the hundreds column. _____

e. Add 7 + 1. _____

f. Write the 1 in 13 above the 3 in the hundreds column. _____

g. Write the 3 in 13 below the line in the tens column. _____

h. Write a 1 below the line in the thousands column. _____

4.   63
    × 7

a. Write the 2 in 21 below the line in the tens column. _____

b. Multiply 7 × 3. _____

c. Multiply 7 × 6. _____

d. Write the 4 in 42 two spaces below the line in the hundreds column. _____

e. Write the 1 in 21 below the line in the ones column. _____

f. Write the 2 in 42 below the 2 in 21 in the tens column. _____

g. Write the 1 in the ones column below the second line in the ones column. _____

h. Draw a line below the 42. _____

i. Add 2 + 2 in the tens column and write the answer below the second line in the tens column. _____

j. Write the 4 in 42 below the second line in the hundreds column. _____

CRITICAL THINKING ACTIVITIES IN PATTERNS, IMAGERY, LOGIC   Dale Seymour Publications

FAVORITE NUMBERS

One fifth-grade teacher asked her students their favorite numbers. Each person in the front row named a different number. Each number was a counting number less than 10. Use the information given below to find out each person's favorite number. Complete the chart. Mark an X in a square when it cannot be the answer. Mark an O to show the favorite number.

1. Bonnie, Victor, and Ruth all chose even numbers.
2. Simon and Dan chose odd numbers.
3. Bonnie's number was less than 4.
4. Victor's number was greater than 6.
5. Ruth's number was three times Bonnie's number.
6. Dan's number was half of Ruth's number.
7. Simon's number was the sum of Bonnie's and Dan's numbers.

Student	1	2	3	4	5	6	7	8	9
Simon									
Bonnie									
Victor									
Dan									
Ruth									

NUMBER SEARCH

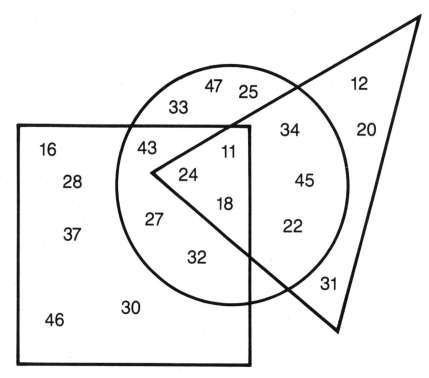

Examples: Which multiples of 3 are in both the triangle and the circle?

___18, 24, 45___

Which multiples of 2 are in the triangle but not in the circle?

___12, 20___

1. Which multiples of 2 are in all three shapes? _____

2. Which multiples of 5 are in the circle but not in the square? _____

3. Which multiples of 3 are in the triangle? _____

4. Which prime numbers are in both the circle and the square? _____

5. Which composite numbers are in neither the square nor the triangle?

_____

6. Which prime number is in the circle but not in the square or the triangle?

_____

7. Which multiples of 2 are in the triangle and the circle but not in the square?

_____

8. Which prime numbers are in the square but not in the triangle? _____

9. Which composite numbers are in the triangle but not in the circle? _____

CRITICAL THINKING ACTIVITIES IN PATTERNS, IMAGERY, LOGIC   Dale Seymour Publications

LOGICAL STRATEGY

Two people play the game of 5-in-a-row. Taking turns, one marks X's, the other marks O's. The first player to mark 5 in a row across, down, or diagonally wins. Answer the questions below each game. Identify the squares by column letters and row numbers.

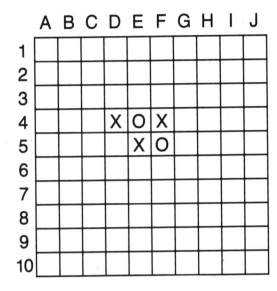

1. It is player O's turn next. Where should player O mark?

_____ or _____

2. Whose turn is next, X's or O's?

_____ Where should this player mark? _____ or _____

3. Where should player X mark next?

_____ or _____

4. Use this grid to play 5-in-a-row with a friend.

STEPS IN ORDER

Listed below are the steps for doing two tasks, but they are not in the proper sequence. Rearrange the steps in the correct order.

1. **Making a peanut butter sandwich**

   a. Lay two pieces of bread on the table.

   b. Remove the lid from the jar of peanut butter.

   c. Eat the sandwich.

   d. Spread peanut butter on one slice of bread.

   e. Remove two pieces of bread from the loaf.

   f. Take a knife from the drawer.

   g. Put the two pieces of bread together to make a sandwich.

   h. Use the knife to remove peanut butter from the jar.

   i. Remove the loaf of bread from the refrigerator.

   j. Remove the jar of peanut butter from the refrigerator.

   k. Wash the dirty knife and put it in the drawer.

   Your order

   ___ ___ ___ ___ ___ ___ ___ ___ ___ ___ ___

2. **Writing and mailing a letter**

   a. Write on the paper with the pen.

   b. Get a pen from the desk.

   c. Take an envelope from the desk.

   d. Fold the letter and insert it in the envelope.

   e. Sit at your desk.

   f. Seal the envelope.

   g. Place the blank paper in front of you.

   h. Mail the letter at the post office.

   i. Place a postage stamp on the envelope.

   j. Take a sheet of blank paper from the desk.

   k. Write the name and address on the envelope.

   Your order

   ___ ___ ___ ___ ___ ___ ___ ___ ___ ___ ___

CRITICAL THINKING ACTIVITIES IN PATTERNS, IMAGERY, LOGIC Dale Seymour Publications

ADDITION AND SUBTRACTION LOGIC

W, X, Y, and Z each stand for a different one-digit number. None of the letters represents zero.

1. Since W + X equals a two-digit number, then Y has

   to be _____. Why? _____

   _____

2. If W is 3, then X is greater than _____. Why?

   _____

3. If Z is 5, then W + X = _____. Why? _____

   _____

4. If Z is 5 and W is 7, then X = _____. Why?

   _____

5. If Z is 7, then W and X have to be which two

   numbers? _____ and _____. Why? _____

   _____

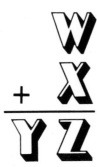

A, B, and C each stand for a different one-digit number. None of the letters stands for zero.

1. What does C + C equal? (Answer in letters.)

   _____

2. Since C is one digit, then A must be what

   number? _____ Why? _____

   _____

   _____

3. Is B odd or even? _____ Why? _____

   _____

   _____

   _____

   _____

4. If C is less than 7, then B is what number? _____

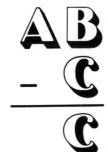

SORTING NUMBERS

★★★

Each of the number disks in the circle belongs in exactly one bucket. Study the pattern for each bucket below, then write the numbers in the bucket and describe the pattern. Make sure you use each number in the circle.

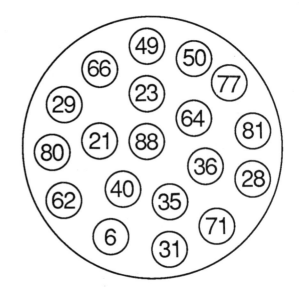

1.

Describe: _____

_____

2.

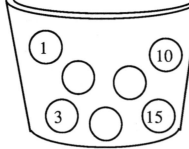

Describe: _____

_____

3.

Describe: _____

_____

4.

Describe: _____

_____

5.

Describe: _____

_____

6.

Describe: _____

_____

CRITICAL THINKING ACTIVITIES IN PATTERNS, IMAGERY, LOGIC   Dale Seymour Publications

DEDUCTIVE LOGIC

Five girls were walking to the park. They were all wearing blouses of different colors. Akiko, Betty, Clara, Dana, and Eve wore blouses that were red, green, blue, white, and yellow (but not necessarily in that order). Use the information given to determine what color blouse each girl wore. Complete the chart. Mark an X in a space when it cannot be the answer. Mark an O to show who wore which blouse.

1. Clara doesn't own a green blouse.

2. Dana hates the colors green and yellow.

3. Betty's blouse was either red or blue.

4. Akiko's blouse was neither green nor white.

5. Clara walked between the girl with the yellow blouse and the girl with the blue blouse.

6. Dana's blouse was red.

	Red	Green	Blue	White	Yellow
Akiko					
Betty					
Clara					
Dana					
Eve					

SETS AND CIRCLES

Write the numbers or letters in the diagram according to the directions. The first one is done as an example.

1. { 2, 7, 9, 11 } are in Circle I.

   { 5, 7, 11, 15 } are in Circle II.

   { 3, 6, 8, 10 } are in neither circle.

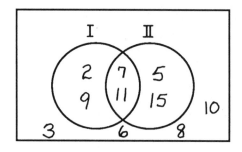

2. { A, B, C, D } are in Circle I.

   { B, D, F, K } are in Circle II.

   { E, G, H } are in neither circle.

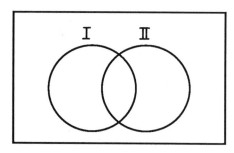

3. { $\frac{1}{2}$, $\frac{2}{3}$, $\frac{9}{10}$, $\frac{11}{12}$, $\frac{4}{7}$, $\frac{8}{11}$ } are in Circle I.

   { $\frac{1}{3}$, $\frac{1}{4}$, $\frac{11}{12}$, $\frac{2}{3}$, $\frac{7}{15}$ } are in Circle II.

   { $\frac{1}{5}$, $\frac{5}{8}$ } are in neither circle.

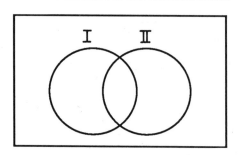

4. The rectangle contains the first nine letters of the alphabet.

   Circle I contains the letters in the word BADGE.

   Circle II contains the letters in the word CHIDE.

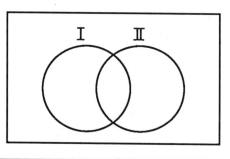

5. Circle I contains the letters in the word FIRST.

   Circle II contains the letters in the word SECOND.

   Circle III contains the letters in the word END.

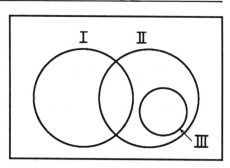

  CRITICAL THINKING ACTIVITIES IN PATTERNS, IMAGERY, LOGIC   Dale Seymour Publications

SHAPE FAMILIES

These are all Pligs.

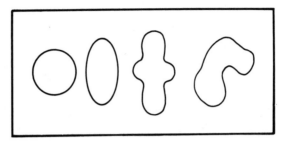

These are not Pligs.

1. Which of the following are Pligs? Draw a ring around each letter.

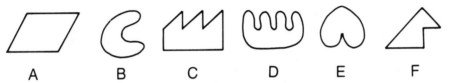

A   B   C   D   E   F

2. What must a Plig have? _____

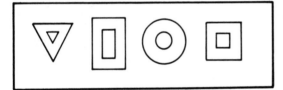

These are all Kloppers.

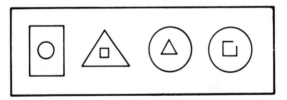

These are not Kloppers.

3. Which of the following are not Kloppers? Draw a ring around each letter.

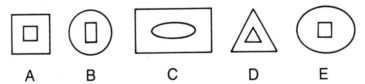

A   B   C   D   E

4. What must a Klopper have? _____

_____

NUMBER LOGIC

Draw a ring around each correct answer.

1. My number is 5 greater than yours.
   Therefore, your number is 5 less than mine.   true   false

2. My number is less than yours.
   Your number is greater than mine.
   Therefore. our numbers are not equal.   true   false

3. My number is twice your number.
   Therefore, your number couldn't be odd.   true   false

4. Three more than your number is 3 less
   than my number.
   Therefore, our numbers are the same.   true   false

5. Kim's number is 2 greater than mine.
   Lou's number is 3 greater than Kim's.
   Therefore, my number is 5 more than Kim's.   true   false

6. Rick's number is an even number.
   Betty's number is an odd number.
   Therefore, Betty's number is greater than Rick's.   true   false

7. My number is twice yours.
   Your number is half of Jo's.
   Therefore, Jo's number is twice mine.   true   false

8. My number is less than yours.
   Your number is greater than Bill's.
   Therefore, Bill's number must be less than mine.   true   false

9. My number is less than 7.
   Your number is greater than 5.
   Therefore, our numbers couldn't be the same.   true   false

10. Brett's number is 3 greater than Bill's.
    Bill's number is 3 less than Sam's.
    Therefore, Sam's number is greater than Brett's.   true   false

CRITICAL THINKING ACTIVITIES IN PATTERNS, IMAGERY, LOGIC   Dale Seymour Publications

MAKE A CHANGE

All of the following sentences are false statements. Make each statement true by changing one word or number, or by removing a word or number. More than one correct answer may be possible for each statement.

1. A prime number has exactly three distinct factors.

2. The sum of two odd numbers is an odd number.

3. The largest odd number that can be formed using all five odd digits is 1 less than 13,580.

4. A triangle has exactly four sides.

5. The sum of 2 three-digit numbers can contain at most five digits.

6. In a division exercise, the dividend is equal to the divisor times the quotient minus the remainder.

7. There are exactly six prime numbers between 30 and 50.

8. The product of 2 two-digit numbers must contain at least two digits.

9. To multiply two fractions, you add the numerators and multiply the denominators.

10. The product of an odd number and an even number is an even number.

11. Twenty-five percent is the same as one-third.

12. The product of 2 three-digit numbers must contain either four or five digits.

13. Using the fewest coins to make 74¢ requires three dimes.

14. The square root of an eight-digit number is at most a five-digit number.

15. The area formula for a circle does not use the irrational number π.

LOGICAL SHAPES

Draw the missing figure or figures to complete each set below.

1. 4 figures: 2 shapes, 2 sizes

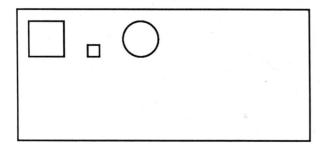

2. 6 figures: 3 shapes, 2 sizes

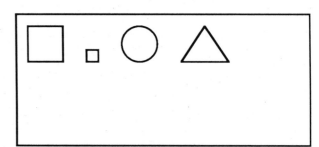

3. 8 figures: 2 shapes, 2 sizes, 2 shades

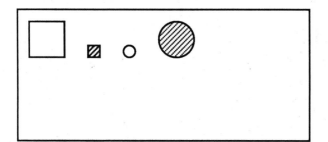

4. 12 figures: 3 shapes, 2 sizes, 2 shades

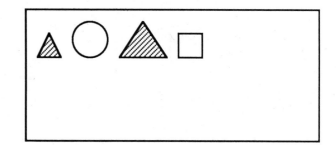

5. 9 figures

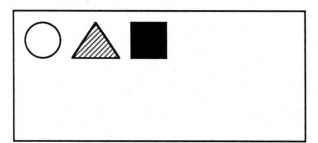

6. 12 figures

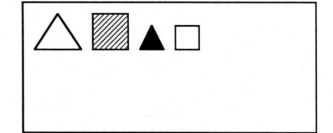

7. 18 figures

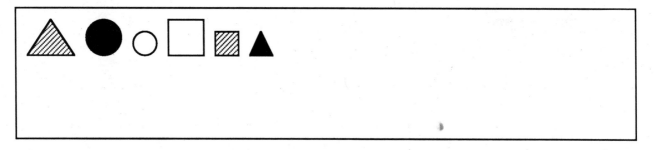

   CRITICAL THINKING ACTIVITIES IN PATTERNS, IMAGERY, LOGIC   Dale Seymour Publications

NUMBER LOGIC

Find the digits that will replace a and b to make the problem correct.

1.
```
   12
   ab
 +79
  145
```
a = _____

b = _____

2.
```
  2,03a
 +b,516
  6,551
```
a = _____

b = _____

3.
```
   8a
  -b7
   59
```
a = _____

b = _____

4.
```
      1a
   b)85
```
a = _____

b = _____

5.
```
   ab
 ×  8
  432
```
a = _____

b = _____

6.
```
   3b
 ×  a
  273
```
a = _____

b = _____

7.
```
   46
   3a
   12
  +bb
  143
```
a = _____

b = _____

8.
```
  321
  2a6
 + 38
  b15
```
a = _____

b = _____

MYSTERY WORDS

Each space represents a letter in a mystery word. Take a blank piece of paper and cover all the clues. Slide the paper down to uncover the first clue. Can you guess the word? Uncover as many clues as you need to figure out the word.

1. ___ ___ ___ ___ ___ ___

    a. The first three letters rhyme with *gum.*

    b. The last three letters mean "cold or frigid."

    c. The first four letters finish this sentence:
       "The dentist makes your face _____ ."

    d. Each of these—1, 2, 3, 4, and 5—is a _____ .

2. ___ ___ ___ ___ ___

    a. There are three vowels (not including I or O).

    b. The last letter is between K and M in the alphabet.

    c. The last two letters form a man's first name.

    d. The second letter is Q.

3. ___ ___ ___ ___ ___ ___ ___

    a. There are four vowels (two A's and two E's).

    b. The last three letters form a word that tells how old you are.

    c. The first three letters are an abbreviation for a type of street (the first letter is A).

    d. The fourth letter is R.

4. ___ ___ ___ ___

    a. There are three vowels.

    b. The first three letters make up the plural form of *is.*

5. ___ ___ ___ ___ ___

    a. There are two vowels (O and I).

    b. The first three letters finish this sentence:
       "A cut tree is a _____ , which is cut into lumber."

    c. The last letter is the third letter in the alphabet.

CRITICAL THINKING ACTIVITIES IN PATTERNS, IMAGERY, LOGIC   Dale Seymour Publications

NUMBER JUGGLING

Write 3, 4, or 12 in each circle to make the number sentences true. Use each number only once in a problem.

1. $\bigcirc + \bigcirc - \bigcirc = 13$

2. $\bigcirc \times \bigcirc - \bigcirc = 0$

3. $\bigcirc - \bigcirc - \bigcirc = 5$

4. $\bigcirc \times \bigcirc + \bigcirc = 24$

5. $\bigcirc \div \bigcirc + \bigcirc = 8$

6. $\bigcirc \div \bigcirc - \bigcirc = 0$

7. $\bigcirc \div \bigcirc \times \bigcirc = 9$

8. $\bigcirc \times \bigcirc \div \bigcirc = 1$

9. $\bigcirc \div \bigcirc \div \bigcirc = 1$

10. $\bigcirc \times \bigcirc \div \bigcirc = 9$

11. $\bigcirc \times \bigcirc - \bigcirc = 32$

LETTER LOGIC

1. I, C, and U each stand for a different single-digit number. None of the letters represents 1. All of the letters represent even numbers. What two problems could the letters represent?

2. W, E, U, and I are either 1, 2, 3, 4, 5, 6, or 7. No two letters represent the same number. WE is even. I is greater than U. What problem do the letters represent?

★Each letter represents a different digit. None of the letters represents zero. Use the facts below to find which number each letter represents.

A	B	C	D	E	F	G	H	I

3. H × H = CH
4. E × E = IE
5. F + F + F + I = E
6. C + C = A
7. A × A = FE
8. D + D = FA
9. D + F = B
10. G + G = FB
11. A + A = B

     CRITICAL THINKING ACTIVITIES IN PATTERNS, IMAGERY, LOGIC   Dale Seymour Publications

ATTRIBUTES

Study the diagram below. Small shapes belong inside the circle that is labeled "small." Shaded shapes belong inside the circle labeled "shaded." Square shapes belong inside the circle labeled "squares." If a shape belongs inside more than one circle, it must have the property of each circle. Write the number of the region where each shape belongs.

Shape   **Region**

1. ◯   _____

2. △   _____

3. ▢   _____

4. ◉   _____

5. ◮   _____

6. ▨   _____

7. ◯   _____

8. △   _____

9. ▢   _____

10. ◉   _____

11. ▲   _____

12. ▨   _____

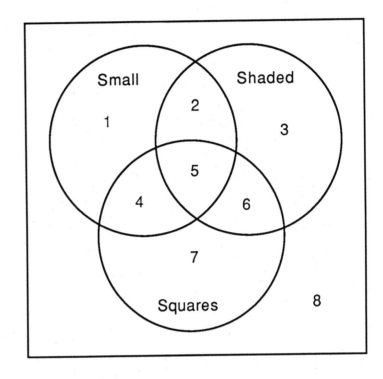

DEDUCTIVE LOGIC

All five students in the first row of Mrs. Martin's math class scored in the 80's on their tests. Use the given information to find out what score each student received. Complete the chart. Mark an X in a space when it cannot be the answer. Mark an O to show the correct score.

1. The scores were 89, 87, 85, 84, and 81.
2. No one in the first row got the same mark.
3. Maria scored higher than Harry and Tulsie.
4. Tulsie scored 84.
5. Ben scored higher than most but not higher than everyone.
6. Maria did not get the highest score in the first row.

	89	87	85	84	81
Maria					
Tulsie					
Ben					
Harry					
Kim					

CRITICAL THINKING ACTIVITIES IN PATTERNS, IMAGERY, LOGIC   Dale Seymour Publications

LOGICAL CONCLUSIONS

Assume that each statement below is true. Write *true, false,* or *can't tell* for each conclusion.

1.   All grungies are troopies.
     No grungies are slopers.
     Flyber is a sloper.

     Conclusion

     a. Flyber is a grungie. _____
     b. Flyber is not a grungie. _____
     c. Flyber is a troopie. _____
     d. Flyber is not a troopie. _____

2.   All grungies are troopies.
     No grungies are slopers.
     Gargol is a grungie.
     Bilgam is a troopie.

     Conclusion

     a. Gargol is a troopie. _____
     b. Gargol is a sloper. _____
     c. Bilgam is a sloper. _____
     d. Bilgam is a troopie. _____
     e. Bilgam and Gargol
        are both troopies. _____
     f. Bilgam and Gargol
        are both grungies. _____

3.   All slurps are flobies.
     No flobies are smitzes.
     Soball is a slurp.
     Switzer is a smitze.
     Floster is a flobie.

     Conclusion

     a. Soball is a smitze. _____
     b. Soball is a flobie. _____
     c. Switzer is a slurp. _____
     d. Switzer is a flobie. _____
     e. Floster is a slurp. _____
     f. Floster is a smitze. _____

DEDUCTIVE REASONING

A list of clubs is given in each exercise below. Study the facts about the clubs. Identify which conclusions are possible by writing *yes* or *no* after each one.

1. **Clubs:** Mosters, Westers
   Facts:
   Jokey is a Moster and a Wester.
   Mokey is a Wester but not a Moster.
   Conclusions:
   a. All Mosters are Westers. _____
   b. All Westers are Mosters. _____
   c. Some Mosters are Westers. ____
   d. Some Westers are Mosters. ____
   e. No Mosters are Westers. _____

2. **Clubs:** Mosters, Westers
   Facts:
   Lokey is a Wester and a Moster.
   Rokey is a Moster but not a Wester.
   Conclusions:
   a. All Mosters are Westers. _____
   b. All Westers are Mosters. _____
   c. Some Mosters are Westers. _____
   d. Some Westers are Mosters. _____
   e. No Mosters are Westers. _____

3. **Clubs:** Mosters, Westers, Olders
   Facts:
   Soaky is a Wester and a Moster.
   Nokey is a Moster but not an Older.
   Dokey is an Older but not a Wester.
   Conclusions:
   a. All Mosters are Westers. _____
   b. All Westers are Mosters. _____
   c. All Westers are Olders. _____
   d. All Olders are Westers. _____
   e. All Mosters are Olders. _____
   f. All Olders are Mosters. _____
   g. No Mosters are Westers. _____
   h. No Westers are Olders. _____
   i. No Mosters are Olders. _____

4. **Clubs:** Mosters, Westers, Olders
   Facts:
   Hokey is not a Wester but is a Moster.
   Koaky is not a Moster but is an Older.
   Pokey is not a Wester but is an Older.
   Conclusions:
   a. All Mosters are Westers. _____
   b. All Westers are Mosters. _____
   c. All Westers are Olders. _____
   d. All Olders are Westers. _____
   e. All Mosters are Olders. _____
   f. All Olders are Mosters. _____
   g. No Mosters are Westers. _____
   h. No Westers are Olders. _____
   i. No Olders are Mosters. _____

CRITICAL THINKING ACTIVITIES IN PATTERNS, IMAGERY, LOGIC   Dale Seymour Publications

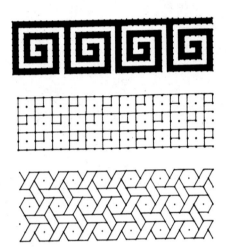

ANSWERS

PART 1: PATTERNS

Page 2, Number Patterns

1.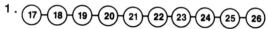

2.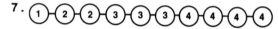

3.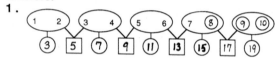

4.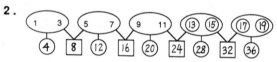

5.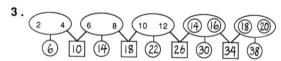

6.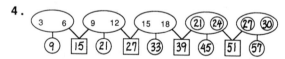

7.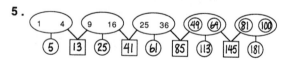

Page 3, Sum Patterns
Descriptions may vary. Accept all correct student answers.

1.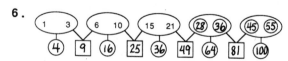

Top row: counting numbers; bottom row: add 2, odd numbers

2.

Top row: odd numbers; bottom row: add 4

3.

Top row: even numbers; bottom row: add 4

4.

Top row: multiples of 3; bottom row: add 6

5.

Top row: numbers squared; bottom row: the difference between the numbers is a multiple of 4

6.

Top row: triangular number; bottom row: numbers squared

Page 4, Number Patterns

1. 2, 4, 6, 8, 10, 12   2. 70, 60, 50, 40, 30, 20

3. 12, 15, 18, 21, 24, 27   4. $9 + 9 = 18$ $9 \times 9 = 81$

5. $24 + 3 = 27$ $24 \times 3 = 72$ 6. a. $47 + 2 = 49$
$47 \times 2 = 94$ b. $497 + 2 = 499$ $497 \times 2 = 994$
c. $4997 + 2 = 4999$ $4997 \times 2 = 9994$
d. $49997 + 2 = 49999$ $49997 \times 2 = 99994$
e. The numbers are reversed.

7. a. $78 + 23 = 101$ b. $778 + 223 = 1001$
c. $7778 + 2223 = 10001$
d. $77778 + 22223 = 100001$
e. $777778 + 222223 = 1000001$ f. Add a zero in the middle each time another digit is added to the addends.   8. a. $12 - 11 = 1$ b. $123 - 111 = 12$
c. $1234 - 1111 = 123$ d. $12345 - 11111 = 1234$
e. $123456 - 111111 = 12345$ f. The answer is the first number in the problem, without the digit in the ones place.

Page 5, Patterns in a Hundreds Chart

1	2	3	4	5	6	7	8	9	10
11	12	13	14	15	16	17	18	19	20
21	22	23	24	25	26	27	28	29	30
31	32	33	34	35	36	37	38	39	40
41	42	43	44	45	46	47	48	49	50
51	52	53	54	55	56	57	58	59	60
61	62	63	64	65	66	67	68	69	70
71	7	73	74	75	76	77	78	79	80
81	82	83	84	85	86	87	88	89	90
91	92	93	94	95	96	97	98	99	100

1. They are multiples of 9.

1	2	3	4	5	6	7	8	9	10
11	12	13	14	15	16	17	18	19	20
21	22	23	24	25	26	27	28	29	30
31	32	33	34	35	36	37	38	39	40
41	42	43	44	45	46	47	48	49	50
51	52	53	54	55	56	57	58	59	60
61	62	63	64	65	66	67	68	69	70
71	72	73	74	75	76	77	78	79	80
81	82	83	84	85	86	87	88	89	90
91	92	93	94	95	96	97	98	99	100

2. They are multiples of 3.

Page 6, Pattern Steps

2.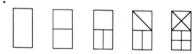

3.

CRITICAL THINKING ACTIVITIES IN PATTERNS, IMAGERY, LOGIC   Dale Seymour Publications

Page 7, Calendar Patterns

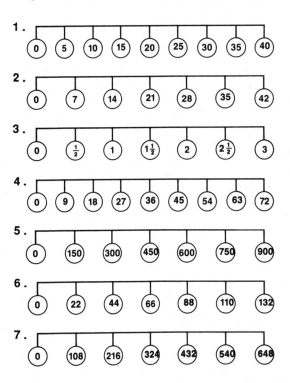

Page 8, Common Property Patterns

1. They are all multiples of 3.   2. The digits in each number are in order.   3. Each second digit is two greater than the first.   4. They are all multiples of 9.

Page 9, Patterns in Shapes

1.

2.

3.

4.

5.

Page 10, Equal Distance Patterns

1. (0) (5) (10) (15) (20) (25) (30) (35) (40)

2. (0) (7) (14) (21) (28) (35) (42)

3. (0) ($\frac{1}{2}$) (1) ($1\frac{1}{2}$) (2) ($2\frac{1}{2}$) (3)

4. (0) (9) (18) (27) (36) (45) (54) (63) (72)

5. (0) (150) (300) (450) (600) (750) (900)

6. (0) (22) (44) (66) (88) (110) (132)

7. (0) (108) (216) (324) (432) (540) (648)

Page 11, Nickel and Dime Patterns

1.

Number of Nickels	1	3	5	7	9
Number of Dimes	4	3	2	1	0

2.

Number of Nickels	0	2	4	6	8	10
Number of Dimes	5	4	3	2	1	0

3.

Number of Nickels	1	3	5	7	9	11
Number of Dimes	5	4	3	2	1	0

4.

Number of Nickels	0	2	4	6	8	10	12
Number of Dimes	6	5	4	3	2	1	0

5. The nickels are either consecutive even numbers or consecutive odd numbers, while the dimes are decreasing consecutive numbers, ending with 0. Also, the sum of each nickel and dime combination increases by one as you go to the right.

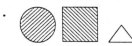

Page 12, Number Table Patterns

1.

1	2	3	4	5	6	7
↓	↓	↓	↓	↓	↓	↓
2	3	4	5	6	7	8

Rule: Add 1.

2.

1	2	3	4	5	6	7
↓	↓	↓	↓	↓	↓	↓
9	10	11	12	13	14	15

Rule: Add 8.

3.

1	2	3	4	5	6	7
↓	↓	↓	↓	↓	↓	↓
3	6	9	12	15	18	21

Rule: Multiply by 3.

4.

10	11	12	13	14	15	16
↓	↓	↓	↓	↓	↓	↓
3	4	5	6	7	8	9

Rule: Subtract 7.

5.

5	1	3	6	7	2	4
↓	↓	↓	↓	↓	↓	↓
30	6	18	36	42	12	24

Rule: Multiply by 6.

Page 13, Letter Combination Patterns

1. 2 words: ON, OF **2.** 2 words: IF, IT
3. 4 words: DOT, DON, DAN, DAB **4.** 4 words:
BIT, BIG, BAG, BAD **5.** 8 combinations: BAIT,
BAIL, BALL, BALT, BELL, BELT, BENT, BEND
6. 8 combinations: CORD, CORE, COME, CAME,
COMP, CAMP, CARP, CARE **7.** 16

Page 14, Design Patterns

1.

2.

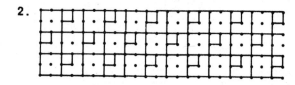

3.

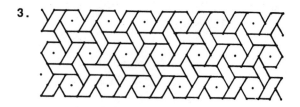

Page 15, Attribute Patterns

Answers will vary. Samples are given below.

1. ⬤ ◼ △

2. ◉ △ ◻

3. △ ◪ △ ◼

4. △ △ △

5. ◯ ⬤ ◻ △

6. ◯ ◻ △ ◯ ◻ △

Page 16, Number Table Patterns

1.

1	2	3	4	5	6	7
↓	↓	↓	↓	↓	↓	↓
8	9	10	11	12	13	14

Rule: Add 7.

2.

15	16	17	18	19	20	21
↓	↓	↓	↓	↓	↓	↓
18	19	20	21	22	23	24

Rule: Add 3.

3.

35	34	33	32	31	30	29
↓	↓	↓	↓	↓	↓	↓
25	24	23	22	21	20	19

Rule: Subtract 10.

4.

4	9	3	12	15	6	100
↓	↓	↓	↓	↓	↓	↓
9	14	8	17	20	11	105

Rule: Add 5.

5.

3	5	7	10	11	14	20
↓	↓	↓	↓	↓	↓	↓
9	15	21	30	33	42	60

Rule: Multiply by 3.

Page 17, Number Patterns

1.  2 — 4 — 6 — 8 — 10 — 12 — 14 — 16 — 18 — 20

2. 3 — 6 — 9 — 12 — 15 — 18 — 21 — 24 — 27 — 30

3. 17 — 27 — 37 — 47 — 57 — 67 — 77 — 87 — 97 — 107 — 117

4.  13 — 15 — 17 — 19 — 21 — 23 — 25 — 27 — 29 — 31 — 33

5. 11 — 22 — 33 — 44 — 55 — 66 — 77 — 88 — 99 — 110

6. 90 — 85 — 80 — 75 — 70 — 65 — 60 — 55 — 50 — 45

7. 101 — 202 — 303 — 404 — 505 — 606 — 707 — 808 — 909 — 1010 — 1111

8. 12 — 23 — 34 — 45 — 56 — 67 — 78 — 89 — 100 — 111 — 122

9. 1 — 8 — 15 — 22 — 29 — 36 — 43 — 50 — 57 — 64

10. 7 — 16 — 25 — 34 — 43 — 52 — 61 — 70 — 79 — 88

Page 18, Calendar Patterns

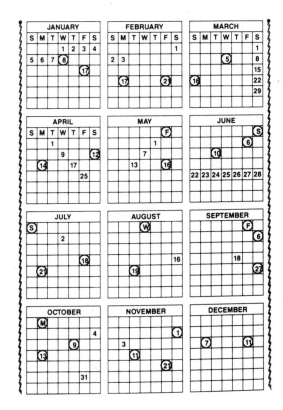

Page 19, Hundreds Chart Patterns

1	2	3	4	5	6	7	8	9	10
11	12	13	14	15	16	17	18	19	20
21	22	23	24	25	26	27	28	29	30
31	32	33	34	35	36	37	38	39	40
41	42	43	44	45	46	47	48	49	50
51	52	53	54	55	56	57	58	59	60
61	62	63	64	65	66	67	68	69	70
71	72	73	74	75	76	77	78	79	80
81	82	83	84	85	86	87	88	89	90
91	92	93	94	95	96	97	98	99	100

1. **They are multiples of 6.**

1	2	3	4	5	6	7	8	9	10
11	12	13	14	15	16	17	18	19	20
21	22	23	24	25	26	27	28	29	30
31	32	33	34	35	36	37	38	39	40
41	42	43	44	45	46	47	48	49	50
51	52	53	54	55	56	57	58	59	60
61	62	63	64	65	66	67	68	69	70
71	72	73	74	75	76	77	78	79	80
81	82	83	84	85	86	87	88	89	90
91	92	93	94	95	96	97	98	99	100

2. **They are multiples of 7.**

Page 20, Even and Odd Patterns

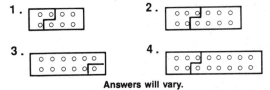

Answers will vary.

The sum of any two even numbers is always an **even** number. Divide the even dot patterns below into two even-number parts.

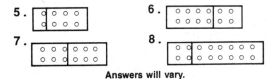

Answers will vary.

9. An even number

10. An odd number

Page 21, Sum Patterns

1.

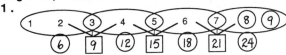

Top row: counting numbers; bottom row: multiples of 3 (or add 3)

2.

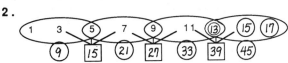

Top row: odd numbers; bottom row: add 6

3.

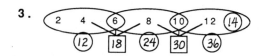

Top row: even numbers; bottom row: add 6 (or multiples of 6)

4.

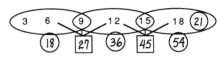

Top row: multiples of 3; bottom row: add 9 (or multiples of 9)

5.

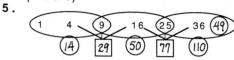

Top row: numbers squared; bottom row: multiples of 3

6.

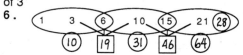

Top row: triangular numbers; bottom row: the difference between the numbers is a multiple of 3

Page 22, Design Patterns

1.

2.

3.

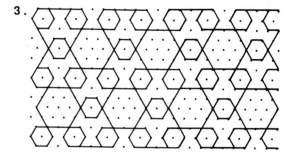

Page 23, Dot and Number Patterns
1.

25   36

2. numbers squared   **3.** yes   **4.** $9 = 1 + 3 + 5$
$16 = 1 + 3 + 5 + 7$ $25 = 1 + 3 + 5 + 7 + 9$
$36 = 1 + 3 + 5 + 7 + 9 + 11$
5.

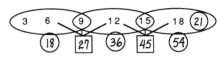

15   21   28

6. $6 = 1 + 2 + 3$ $10 = 1 + 2 + 3 + 4$
$15 = 1 + 2 + 3 + 4 + 5$ $21 = 1 + 2 + 3 + 4 + 5 + 6$
7. Triangular numbers: add the next consecutive number to the previous sum

Page 24, Digit Combination Patterns

1. 2 numbers: 23, 25   **2.** 4 numbers: 357, 352, 362, 361   **3.** 4 numbers: 451, 452, 462, 468
4. 8 numbers: 1379, 1376, 1326, 1325, 1426, 1425, 1485, 1480   **5.** 8 numbers: 9863, 9862, 9852, 9851, 9752, 9751, 9741, 9740   **6.** 16 numbers: 14685, 14687, 14657, 14653, 14257, 14253, 14203, 14202, 19257, 19253, 19203, 19202, 19103, 19102, 19132, 19134
7.

How many digits in each number?	2	3	4	5	6	7	8
How many numbers?	2	4	8	16	32	64	128

Page 25, Product Patterns

1.
```
      11
    × 11
      01
    0101
    + 01
     121
```

2.
```
     111
   × 111
     01
    0101
   010101
    0101
     01
   12321
```

3.
```
      1111
    × 1111
       01
      0101
     010101
    01010101
     010101
      0101
       01
    1234321
```

4.
```
      55
    × 55
      25
    2525
      25
    3025
```

5.
```
      555
    × 555
       25
     2525
   252525
     2525
       25
   308025
```

6.
```
       5555
     × 5555
         25
       2525
     252525
   25252525
     252525
       2525
         25
   30858025
```

7.
```
      44
    × 33
      12
    1212
    + 12
    1452
```

8.
```
      444
    × 333
       12
     1212
   121212
     1212
     + 12
   147852
```

9. Answers will vary. Accept all correct student answers.

CRITICAL THINKING ACTIVITIES IN PATTERNS, IMAGERY, LOGIC   Dale Seymour Publications

Page 26, Common Property Patterns
1. They are all multiples of 7. **2.** The numbers read the same backwards as forwards; they are palindromes. **3.** The digits add up to 8. **4.** They are multiples of 12.

Page 27, Product Patterns
1. They are multiples of 4. **2.** They are multiples of 5. **3.** They are perfect squares. **4.** They are powers or 3. **5.** Answers may vary. One possibility: The products of the diagonal numbers in the square are equal. **6.** In any row the sum of the number in column **1** and the number in column **2** equals the number in column **3**. Other solutions are possible. Accept all correct student answers. For example: The sum of the number in column 2 and the number in column 3 equals the number in column 5. **7.** Answers will vary. Accept all correct student answers.

Page 28, Even and Odd Patterns

1.

B	I	N	G	O
7	18	40	60	72
11	29	33	58	67
9	17	free	52	65
6	23	35	50	73
3	25	41	48	61

2.

B	I	N	G	O
11	20	34	52	66
6	28	37	60	61
2	18	free	55	72
10	24	44	48	70
14	25	38	56	64

3.

B	I	N	G	O
7	18	41	55	67
3	21	35	48	71
15	29	free	59	72
6	27	44	49	65
1	23	33	60	73

Page 29, Special Number Patterns
1. $1089 \times 1 = 1089$ $1089 \times 2 = 2178$
$1089 \times 3 = 3267$ $1089 \times 4 = 4356$ $1089 \times 5 = 5445$
$1089 \times 6 = 6534$ $1089 \times 7 = 7623$ $1089 \times 8 = 8712$
$1089 \times 9 = 9801$ The numbers in the thousands and the hundreds places are increasing consecutive numbers, while the numbers in the tens and ones places are decreasing consecutive numbers.

2. $1 \times 8 + 1 = 9$ $12 \times 8 + 2 = 98$ $123 \times 8 + 3 = 987$
$1234 \times 8 + 4 = 9876$ $12345 \times 8 + 5 = 98765$
$123456 \times 8 + 6 = 987654$ $1234567 \times 8 + 7 = 9876543$
$12345678 \times 8 + 8 = 98765432$ The answer increases by one place each time, and each new place value is the next lower consecutive number.

3. $3367 \times 33 = 111,111$ $3367 \times 66 = 222,222$
$3367 \times 99 = 333,333$ $3367 \times 132 = 444,444$
$3367 \times 165 = 555,555$ $3367 \times 198 = 666,666$
$3367 \times 231 = 777,777$ Each digit in the answers increases by 1 (or add 111,111 each time).

4. $1 \times 9 + 2 = 11$ $12 \times 9 + 3 = 111$
$123 \times 9 + 4 = 1111$ $1234 \times 9 + 5 = 11,111$
$12345 \times 9 + 6 = 111,111$ $123456 \times 9 + 7 = 1,111,111$
$1234567 \times 9 + 8 = 11,111,111$ Add another place to each answer, and all digits are 1's. The addend gives you the number of digits in each answer. **5.** yes; multiply first

Page 30, Number Patterns

1.
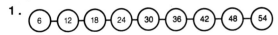
6 — 12 — 18 — 24 — 30 — 36 — 42 — 48 — 54

2.
18 — 25 — 32 — 39 — 46 — 53 — 60 — 67 — 74 — 81

3.
99 — 97 — 95 — 93 — 91 — 89 — 87 — 85 — 83

4.
7 — 14 — 21 — 28 — 35 — 42 — 49 — 56 — 63 — 70

5.
101 — 212 — 323 — 434 — 545 — 656 — 767 — 878 — 989

6.
19 — 28 — 37 — 46 — 55 — 64 — 73 — 82 — 91 — 100

7.
1 — 2 — 4 — 8 — 16 — 32 — 64 — 128 — 256

8.
10 — 20 — 40 — 70 — 110 — 160 — 220 — 290 — 370 — 460

Page 31, Addend Patterns
$4 = 0 + 4 = 1 + 3 = 2 + 2$
$5 = 0 + 5 = 1 + 4 = 2 + 3$; 3 addends
$6 = 0 + 6 = 1 + 5 = 2 + 4 = 3 + 3$; 4 addends
$7 = 0 + 7 = 1 + 6 = 2 + 5 = 3 + 4$; 4 addends
$8 = 0 + 8 = 1 + 7 = 2 + 6 = 3 + 5 = 4 + 4$; 5 addends
$9 = 0 + 9 = 1 + 8 = 2 + 7 = 3 + 6 = 4 + 5$; 5 addends
$10 = 0 + 10 = 1 + 9 = 2 + 8 = 3 + 7 = 4 + 6 = 5 + 5$;
6 addends

14	15	16	17	20	21	50	100
8	8	9	9	11	11	26	51

Even numbers: consecutive counting numbers beginning with 2
Odd numbers: consecutive counting numbers

Page 32, Winning Patterns
1. The player having the larger even number.
2. The player having the smaller odd number.

Page 33, Calendar Patterns

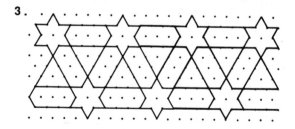

(Calendar grid for all twelve months: JANUARY, FEBRUARY, MARCH, APRIL, MAY, JUNE, JULY, AUGUST, SEPTEMBER, OCTOBER, NOVEMBER, DECEMBER with circled dates.)

Page 34, Letter Combination Patterns

1. 8 paths   2. 2 paths   3. 4 paths   4. 8 paths
5. 16 paths   6. Answers will vary. Accept all correct student answers.
7.

Number of letters in each word	2	3	4	5	6	7	8
Number of paths	2	4	8	16	32	64	128

Page 35, Patterns and Rules

1.

5	6	7	8	9	10	11
↓	↓	↓	↓	↓	↓	↓
14	15	16	**17**	**18**	**19**	**20**

Rule: Add 9.

2.

13	20	15	7	12	50	100
↓	↓	↓	↓	↓	↓	↓
9	16	**11**	**3**	**8**	**46**	**96**

Rule: Subtract 4.

3.

5	17	9	11	25	31	100
↓	↓	↓	↓	↓	↓	↓
10	34	18	**22**	**50**	**62**	**200**

Rule: Multiply by 2.

4.

9	5	15	8	11	13	100
↓	↓	↓	↓	↓	↓	↓
45	25	75	**40**	**55**	**65**	**500**

Rule: Multiply by 5.

5.

1	2	3	4	5	6	7
↓	↓	↓	↓	↓	↓	↓
3	5	7	9	**11**	**13**	**15**

Rule: Multiply by 2 and add 1.

Page 36, Counting Squares Patterns

1.

Size of Square	Number of Squares With: 1-Square Unit	4-Square Unit	9-Square Unit	16-Square Unit	25-Square Unit	36-Square Unit	Total Number of Squares
1 × 1	1						1
2 × 2	4	1					5
3 × 3	9	4	1				14
4 × 4	16	9	4	1			30
5 × 5	25	16	9	4	1		55
6 × 6	36	25	16	9	4	1	91

2. Answers will vary. Accept all correct student answers.   3. Add all the perfect squares from 1 to 100.

Page 37, Common Property Patterns

1. They are multiples of 8.   2. The sum of the digits for each number is 9.   3. The digits of each number differ by 4.   4. They are multiples of 6.

Page 38, Paper Strip Patterns

1. d. one large loop   2. 2 interconnected loops: 1 large and 1 small   3. 2 large interconnected loops
4. 3 interconnected loops: 2 large and 1 small
5. 3 large interconnected loops
6.

Number of Cuts	1	2	3	4	5	6	7	8
Number of Large Loops	1	1	2	2	3	3	4	4
Number of Small Loops	0	1	0	1	0	1	0	1

Page 39, Design Patterns

1.

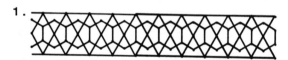

2.

3.

(Triangular and star tessellation pattern.)

Page 40, Number Patterns

1. 1976, 1980, 1984, 1988, 1992, 1996; add 4
2. 91, 82, 73, 64, 55, 46, 37, 28, 19; subtract 9
3. 1, 10, 100, 1000, 10,000, 100,000; powers of 10
4. 37, 41, 45, 49, 53, 57, 61, 65; add 4
5. 121, 232, 343, 454, 565, 676; add 111   **6.** 117, 126, 135, 144, 153, 162, 171, 180, 189; add 9
7. 12, 24, 36, 48, 510, 612, 714, 816; first part of number formed by counting by ones, second part formed by counting by twos   **8.** 1, 4, 9, 16, 25, 36, 49, 64; perfect squares   **9.** 1, 8, 27, 81, 243, 729; powers of 3   **10.** 1, 3, 6, 10, 15, 21, 28, 36; triangular numbers

Page 41, BINGO Patterns

1.

B	I	N	G	O
10	20	42	53	70
7	25	43	52	75
⑨	⑯	free	㊾	㊻
12	22	34	57	61
18	24	35	46	68

2.

B	I	N	G	O
4	18	42	46	61
13	24	35	52	68
10	20	free	49	64
12	16	34	57	75
7	25	43	53	70

3.

B	I	N	G	O
4	25	42	57	64
9	24	46	53	73
10	18	free	50	68
18	20	31	46	75
2	30	49	48	70

Page 42, Error Patterns

1. 14 + 38 = 42   39 + 47 = 76; The student didn't carry the 1 over to the tens place.
2. 365 − 189 = 224; 472 − 148 = 336; The student always subtracted the smaller number from the larger number.   **3.** 5004 − 2329 = 1785; 7003 − 2148 = 2965; The student borrowed a 1 from the left each time a larger number was needed, instead of just once.   **4.** 26 × 4 = 164; 76 × 8 = 888; The student added the number in the tens place to the number that was carried over, then multiplied.

Page 43, Logic Patterns

1.

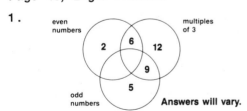

Answers will vary.

2. Set A has even numbers.   **3.** Set B has multiples of 3.   **4.** Set C has multiples of 5.
5. It has multiples of 3 and 5.   **6.** It has even numbers that are multiples of 5.   **7.** It has even numbers that are multiples of 3 and 5.

Page 44, Pattern Search

1. 5   **2.** 13   **3. a.** 97, row I   **b.** 972, row I   **c.** 9725, row I   **d.** 98742, row D   **e.** 987425, row D   **f.** 9725608, row I   **g.** 98742513, row D   **h.** 947132568, row G   **4.** Row A: 25; Row B: 64; Row C: 36; Row D: 25; Row E: 25, 49; Row F: 64, 81; Row G: 25; Row H: 49; Row I: 25; Row J: 36
5. Row A: 84; Row B: 91; Row C: 84; Row D: 98; Row E: 56; Row F: 42; Row G: 56; Row H: 49; Row I: 56   **6.** 0; because 0 appears in each row
7. 9168619   **8.** Answers will vary. Accept all correct student answers.

Page 45, Number Chain Patterns

Answers may vary. Suggestions are shown below. Accept all correct student answers.

1.

	J	K	L	M	N	O	P	Q	R	S
A	1	3	0	8	4	6	9	2	5	7
B	0	2	5	7	9	1	3	8	6	4
C	5	9	1	3	6	8	4	0	2	7
D	6	0	9	8	7	4	2	5	1	3
E	2	5	6	7	0	8	1	3	4	9
F	8	1	3	8	5	7	0	6	4	2
G	9	4	7	1	3	2	5	6	8	0
H	2	4	9	0	7	6	1	3	8	5
I	9	7	2	5	6	0	8	1	3	4
J	4	1	3	6	7	5	8	2	0	9

2.

	J	K	L	M	N	O	P	Q	R	S
A	1	3	0	8	4	6	9	2	5	7
B	0	2	5	7	9	1	3	8	6	4
C	5	9	1	3	6	8	4	0	2	7
D	6	0	9	8	7	4	2	5	1	3
E	2	5	6	7	0	8	1	3	4	9
F	8	1	3	9	5	7	0	6	4	2
G	9	4	7	1	3	2	5	6	8	0
H	2	4	9	0	7	6	1	3	8	5
I	9	7	2	5	6	0	8	1	3	4
J	4	1	3	6	7	5	8	2	0	9

3.

	J	K	L	M	N	O	P	Q	R	S
A	1	3	0	8	4	6	9	2	5	7
B	0	2	5	7	9	1	3	8	6	4
C	5	9	1	3	6	8	4	0	2	7
D	6	0	9	8	7	4	2	5	1	3
E	2	5	6	7	0	8	1	3	4	9
F	8	1	3	9	5	7	0	6	4	2
G	9	4	7	1	3	2	5	6	8	0
H	2	4	9	0	7	6	1	3	8	5
I	9	7	2	5	6	0	8	1	3	4
J	4	1	3	6	7	5	8	2	0	9

4.

	J	K	L	M	N	O	P	Q	R	S
A	1	3	0	8	4	6	9	2	5	7
B	0	2	5	7	9	1	3	8	6	4
C	5	9	1	3	6	8	4	0	2	7
D	6	0	9	8	7	4	2	5	1	3
E	2	5	6	7	0	8	1	3	4	9
F	8	1	3	9	5	7	0	6	4	2
G	9	4	7	1	3	2	5	6	8	0
H	2	4	9	0	7	6	1	3	8	5
I	9	7	2	5	6	0	8	1	3	4
J	4	1	3	6	7	5	8	2	0	9

Page 46, Special Number Patterns

1. $16 + 17 + 18 + 19 + 20 = 21 + 22 + 23 + 24$;
$25 + 26 + 27 + 28 + 29 + 30 = 31 + 32 + 33 + 34 + 35$;
$36 + 37 + 38 + 39 + 40 + 41 + 42 = 43 + 44 + 45 + 46 + 47 + 48$

Descriptions will vary. Accept all correct student answers.

2. $7^2 = 4 + 5 + 6 + 7 + 8 + 9 + 10$
$9^2 = (2 \times 5 - 1)^2 = 5 + 6 + 7 + 8 + 9 + 10 + 11 + 12 + 13$
$11^2 = (2 \times 6 - 1)^2 = 6 + 7 + 8 + 9 + 10 + 11 + 12 + 13 + 14 + 15 + 16$

Descriptions will vary. Accept all correct student answers.

PART 2: IMAGERY

Page 54, Dot Designs

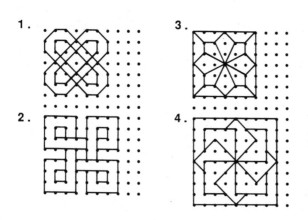

Page 55, Order by Size

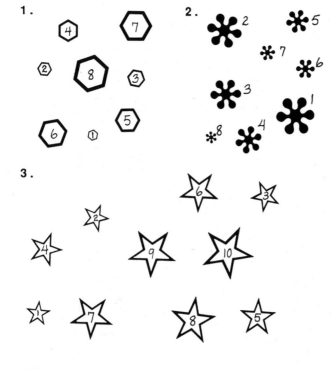

Page 56, Perception Puzzle

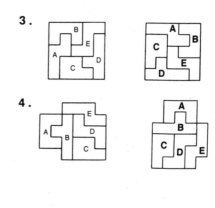

Page 57, Comparing Shapes

1. A and H, C and G   **2.** C

Page 58, Symmetry Symbols
1. A, B, D, E, H, I, J

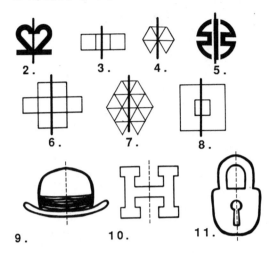

2.   3.   4.   5.

6.   7.   8.

9.   10.   11.

Page 59, Match and Patch
A–2, B–8, C–7, D–1, E–3, F–5, G–6, H–4

Page 60, Cut-Ups
1. B   2. A, E   3. C, D   4. B, E

Page 61, Puzzle Shapes

1.

2.

3.

Page 62, Match the Patch

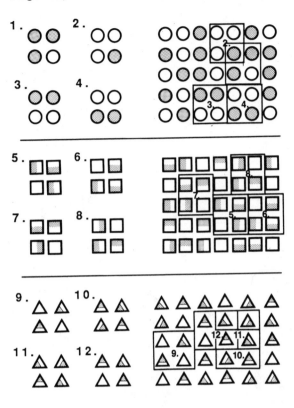

1.   2.

3.   4.

5.   6.

7.   8.

9.   10.

11.   12.

Page 63, Cube Patterns
1. A, D   2. B, C   3. A, B   4. B, D

Page 64, Mirror Images
1. FOR SALE   2. PHARMACY   3. GASOLINE

4. ONE WAY

5. ICE CREAM   6. AMBULANCE

7. THANK YOU   8. MOVIES

Page 65, Parts of a Whole
1. B   2. A   3. C   4. A

Page 66, Cube Patterns
1. B   2. A   3. D   4. B

Page 67, Designs on Dots

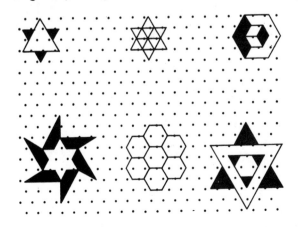

Page 68, Order by Size

1.

2.

3.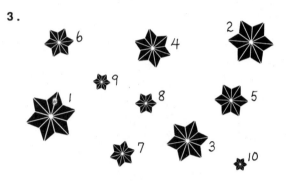

Page 69, Picture Puzzle

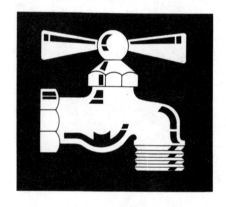

Page 70, Comparing Designs
1. D   2. A   3. D and E   4. B and E   5. A

Page 71, Puzzle Shapes
1. F   2. M   3. K   4. G   5. E   6. D   7. B
8. N   9. C   10. L   11. A   12. H   13. I
14. O   15. J   16. P

Page 72, Comparing Designs
1. D   2. C   3. E   4. B

Page 73, Mirror Images

1.   2.   3.   4.

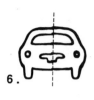 

5.   6.   7.

8. A, C, D, F, G, J, L, M

Page 74, Cube Patterns
1. B, C   2. A, D   3. A, B, D   4. C or D

Page 75, Stare and Compare
1. E   2. C   3. G and I, E and J

Page 76, Reading Backwards
1. Home, sweet home.   2. Hickory, Dickory, Dock
3. Look before you leap.   4. To be or not to be . . .
5. Rain, rain go away.   6. A penny saved is a
penny earned.   7. Early to bed, early to rise.
8. All's well that ends well.   9. Life, liberty and the
pursuit of happiness.   10. Time is money.
11. Who's afraid?   12. A dog is man's best friend.

Page 77, Cube Views
1. a. 4 b. 3 c. 6 2. a. 3 b. 2 c. 4
3. a. A b. D c. E 4. a. C b. D c. E

Page 78, Pattern Puzzles

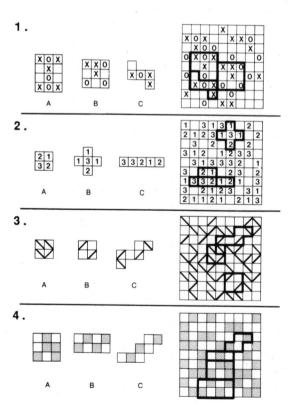

1.

2.

3.

4.

CRITICAL THINKING ACTIVITIES IN PATTERNS, IMAGERY, LOGIC   Dale Seymour Publications

Page 79, Lines and Designs

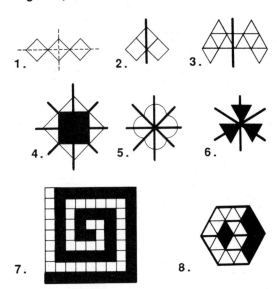

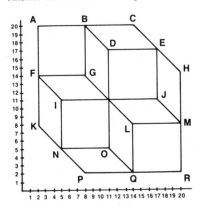

Page 80, Circular Reasoning
1. L 2. B 3. E 4. D 5. K 6. H
7. F or L 8. I 9. G 10. A

Page 81, Folded Shapes
1. C 2. D 3. B 4. D

Page 82, Picture Plotting

Answer will resemble this figure.

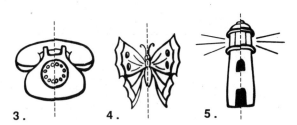

Page 83, Mirror Images
1. A, C, F, I, J, K, M 2. B,

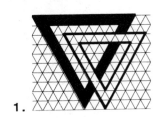

Page 84, Grid Designs

Page 85, Puzzle Parts

Page 86, Parts of a Whole
1. D 2. D 3. A 4. C 5. C 6. E 7. D
8. E 9. E 10. B 11. A 12. A 13. B
14. B and C

Page 87, Creative Bisecting
Answers will vary. Accept all correct student answers.

Page 88, Puzzle Shapes
1. N 2. B 3. H 4. F 5. L 6. A 7. J
8. I 9. C 10. P 11. K 12. G 13. O
14. D 15. M 16. E

Page 89, Grids and Symmetry

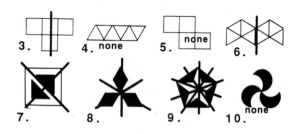

3. 4. none 5. none 6.

7. 8. 9. 10. none

Page 90, Crazy Shapes
1. E   2. A and H

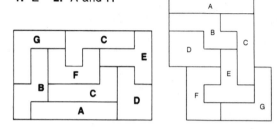

Page 91, Comparing Designs
1. D   2. C   3. C and E   4. A and E

Page 92, Fine Lines

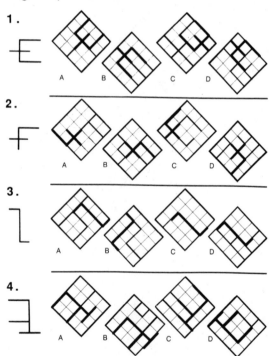

Page 93, Mirror Drawings
Accept all correct student drawings of mirror images.

Page 94, Reading Backwards
1. Absence makes the heart grow fonder. 2. Two's company, three's a crowd. 3. Dr. Livingston, I presume. 4. All for one, one for all. 5. Little strokes, fell great oaks. 6. All men are created equal. 7. A picture is worth a thousand words. 8. Don't put all your eggs in one basket.

Page 95, Directional Turns

	A	B	C	D	E
1.	CW	CCW	CW	CCW	
	CCW	CW	CCW	CW	
2.	CW	CCW	CW	CCW	CW
	CW	CCW	CW	CCW	CW
3.	CW	CW	CCW	CCW	
4.	CW	CCW	CCW	CW	

Page 96, Folded Shapes
1. B   2. A   3. B   4. B

Page 97, Parts of a Whole
1. A, B, D   2. A, C, D   3. A, B, F   4. B, C, E
5. A, B, D

Page 98, Cube Views

1. a. ⬡ b. ◇ c. ⌒ 2. a. △ b. ⌒
c. ◇ 3. a. ⊡ b. ⊡ c. ⊡
4. a. ⊡ b. ⊡ c. ⊡

Page 99, Hidden Shapes

Page 100, Cube Patterns
1. A, C   2. A, C, D   3. B, D   4. A, B, C

CRITICAL THINKING ACTIVITIES IN PATTERNS, IMAGERY, LOGIC   Dale Seymour Publications

Page 101, Points and Lines

Answers may vary.

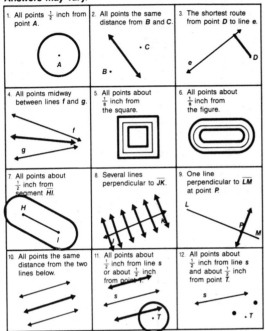

1. All points $\frac{1}{2}$ inch from point A.
2. All points the same distance from B and C.
3. The shortest route from point D to line e.
4. All points midway between lines f and g.
5. All points about $\frac{1}{8}$ inch from the square.
6. All points about $\frac{1}{8}$ inch from the figure.
7. All points about $\frac{1}{2}$ inch from segment HI.
8. Several lines perpendicular to $\overline{JK}$.
9. One line perpendicular to $\overline{LM}$ at point P.
10. All points the same distance from the two lines below.
11. All points about $\frac{1}{2}$ inch from line s or about $\frac{1}{2}$ inch from point T.
12. All points about $\frac{1}{2}$ inch from line s and about $\frac{1}{2}$ inch from point T.

Page 102, Illusions

Answer will resemble this figure.

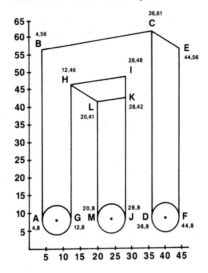

PART 3: LOGIC

Page 104, Strings Attached
1. 4 balloons   2. 2 balloons   3. 2 balloons
4. 3 balloons   5. 1 balloon   6. 2 balloons
7. 3 balloons   8. 4 balloons

Page 105, Oh Brother!
1. Dave   2. Dan   3. Dick   4. Don   5. Dan

Page 106, Moo-ving Logic
1. Bessie, Flossie, Sadie, Daisy   2. Moozie, Suzie, Lucy, Belle   3. Flossie, Daisy, Suzie, Belle
4. Bessie, Flossie, Moozie, Suzie   5. Sadie, Daisy, Lucy, Belle   6. Sadie, Lucy   7. Moozie
8. Daisy   9. Flossie, Suzie   10. Belle

Page 107, Number Sense
1. false   2. false   3. true   4. true   5. false
6. true   7. true

Page 108, Locating Letters
1. R   2. S   3. W   4. F   5. W   6. A   7. M
8. Y   9. U   10. E

Page 109, Letter Logic
A − 2 = B
1. 7   2. 2   3. 7   4. 12   5. A − B = 2
X × Y = Z
1. 15   2. 8   3. 4   4. 4   5. Answers will vary:
7 or 5; 1 or 35

Page 110, Sets and Circles
1. A   2. C   3. B   4. D   5. A   6. D   7. C
8. B   9. A   10. C   11. D   12. B

Page 111, Comparing Symbols
1. C   2. D   3. A and B   4. Answers will vary.
A Dean must have the same shape, in the same position, on either side. One shape will be filled in and the other will be open.

Page 112, State-A-Date
1. April 2, 9, 16, 30   2. February 3, 10, 17, 24
3. August 5, 19, 26   4. January 4, 11, 18, 25
5. September 2, 9, 16, 23, 30   6. May 5, 12, 19, 26
7. November 4, 11, 18, 25   8. March 7, 14, 21, 28
9. January 1, 8, 15, 22, 29   10. October 3, 10, 17, 24

Page 113, Order Sorter
A. math 6 + 8 = 14 end   B. Is this all?
C. Mathematics is the study of powerful, exciting and useful ideas.
D. One, two, Hear the cow moo.
Three, four, I hope there's no more.
Five, six, Fiddlesticks.

Page 114, Table Logic
1. Mr. Sanchez   2. Isabel   3. Maria   4. Juan
5. Mr. Sanchez   6. Ramon   7. Ramon
8. Mrs. Sanchez

Page 115, Letter Perfect
1. C A T D O K L   2. M A D E B N T C
3. T O U R S P Y M C B   4. F A C T O R M H I N
5. A N G L E P I T R   6. E Q U A L S R O N T
7. D I S T A N C E G R M L
8. E Q U A T I O N F R M L C B S

9. R A T I O S C U E V L M
10. Z E R O D C I M A L U T P

Page 116, Number Sentences
1. $5-4=1$ 2. $4-2=2$ 3. $5-2=3$
4. $2+4-5=1$ 5. $5+2-4=3$ 6. $5+4-2=7$
7. $4\times2-5=3$ 8. $5\times2-4=6$ 9. $5\times4-2=18$

Page 117, Favorite Games
1. 1 2. 7 3. 2 4. 6 5. 5

Page 118, Educated Guesses
1. 6; 14; 32; even 2. 16; 104; 28; even
3. 15; 33; 71; odd 4. 6; 14; 28; even 5. 4;
12; 36; even 6. 3; 11; 27; odd 7. 12; 136;
128; even 8. 9; 77; 75; odd 9. even 10. odd
11. even 12. odd 13. even 14. odd

Page 119, Letter Logic
A + 3 = B
1. 8 2. 7 3. 6 4. 3
X + Y + 2 = Z
1. 6 2. 9 3. 5 4. 4 5. 5

Page 120, Shifting Digits
1. $92-86$ 2. $654-13$ 3. $134-65$
4. $864-123$ 5. $412-386$ 6. 56×3 7. 53×6
8. 32×81

Page 121, Finding Figures

	Number
Hexagon and pentagons in all	3
Squares inside circles	2
Circles inside squares	1
Triangles inside the octagon	1
Circles not inside circles	2
Polygons in all	11
Polygons not inside circles	6
Polygons inside circles	5

Page 122, Finding Numbers
1. 57 2. 37 3. 27, 51, 57 4. 57 5. 53, 97
6. 75 7. 27 8. 39

Page 123, Five-in-a-Row
1. D5 2. C8 or G4 3. O's

Page 124, How to Solve It
1. add the numbers, subtract the numbers
2. choose the larger number 3. multiply the
numbers, subtract the numbers 4. choose the
smaller number 5. add the numbers, subtract the
numbers 6. subtract the numbers 7. divide the
numbers 8. multiply the numbers, add the numbers
9. subtract the numbers, divide the numbers
10. subtract the numbers, divide the numbers

Page 125, Letter Logic
A + B = C
1. 6 or 8 2. 7, 9 3. 4 or 8 4. 5 5. 6 6. 6

X + Y = Z
1. 9; 9 is the greatest one-digit number 2. 8; If X
were 8 and Y were 1, Z would be 9, which is the largest
one-digit number. 3. 3; 2 + 1 = 3; This is the
smallest combination possible since all numbers are
different. 4. 1; If Y were 0, then Z would equal X,
and each number stands for a different number.

Page 126, Code Feat
1. 13 2. 3 3. 1 4. 36 5. 6 6. 4 7. 5
8. 50 9. 25 10. 21 11. 24 12. 9 13. 25
14. 18 15. 5

Page 127, Favorite Subject

Student	Reading	Art	Math	Writing
Bill	X	X	X	O
Sally	O	X	X	X
Bob	X	X	O	X
Sue	X	O	X	X

Page 128, Outside In
1. a. 3, 4, 6, 7 b. 2, 3, 4, 5 c. 2, 4 d. 3, 1, 6
e. 5 2. a. 3 b. 5 c. 7 3. a. C, H, G, F
b. C, B, D, G c. D d. H, C, F, A 4. a. H
b. D c. E

Page 129, Design Codes
1. Baa: C, E, F, H 2. Dokos: A, C, D, H

Page 130, Over Herd
1. Sadie 2. Suzie 3. Moozie 4. Daisy
5. Bessie 6. Belle 7. Suzie 8. Flossie and
Lucy 9. Bessie and Daisy

Page 131, Number Sentences
Answers may vary. Suggestions follow, but accept all
correct student answers.
1. $3+5=8$; $9-7=2$ 2. $2+4=6$; $8-7=1$;
$3\times5=15$ 3. $3+7=10$; $20-9=11$; $2\times8=16$
4. $4+11=15$; $60-24=36$; $6\times7=42$; $72\div8=9$

Page 132, Number Sense
1. false 2. true 3. false 4. true 5. true
6. true 7. true

Page 133, Rhyme Tyme
1. two 2. multiply 3. geometry 4. percent
5. metric 6. divide 7. prime 8. triangle
9. sum 10. subtract

Page 134, Digit Doings
1. $x=3$; $y=6$ 2. $x=5$; $y=7$ 3. $x=9$; $y=8$
4. $x=2$; $y=6$ 5. $x=3$; $y=2$ 6. $x=1$; $y=3$
7. $x=5$; $y=7$

Page 135, Letter Perfect
1. T 2. T 3. T 4. F 5. F 6. F 7. T
8. T 9. T 10. F 11. T 12. T 13. F
14. T 15. T 16. F 17. T 18. T 19. F
20. F

Page 136, Number Shuffle

In some cases, the order of these numbers may vary.
1. $2 + 3 + 6 = 11$ **2.** $6 + 3 - 2 = 7$ **3.** $6 + 2 - 3 = 5$
4. $6 \times 3 + 2 = 20$ **5.** $6 \times 2 + 3 = 15$
6. $2 \times 3 + 6 = 12$ **7.** $6 \times 3 - 2 = 16$
8. $6 \times 2 - 3 = 9$ **9.** $2 \times 3 - 6 = 0$ **10.** $6 \times 3 \div 2 = 9$

Page 137, Letter Logic

A + B = CD
1. 1 **2.** 7 or 9 **3.** 8 or 9 **4.** 8 **5.** D can't
be 1 because C must be 1, and all the numbers are
different.
W + X + Y = Z
1. 9 **2.** 4 **3.** 4 **4.** 9 **5.** 6; All numbers have
to be different. The smallest sum possible is $1 + 2 + 3$.

Page 138, Order Sorter

The correct order is given in each of the following
answers.
1. E, C, A, F, B, D, G **2.** E, B, A, G, F, C, D, H
3. C, E, A, F, B, D **4.** B, E, A, C, F, D, H, G, I, J

Page 139, Favorite Numbers

Student	1	2	3	4	5	6	7	8	9
Simon	X	X	X	X	O	X	X	X	X
Bonnie	X	O	X	X	X	X	X	X	X
Victor	X	X	X	X	X	X	X	O	X
Dan	X	X	O	X	X	X	X	X	X
Ruth	X	X	X	X	X	O	X	X	X

Page 140, Number Search

1. 18, 24 **2.** 25, 45 **3.** 12, 18, 24, 45 **4.** 11,
43 **5.** 25, 33 **6.** 47 **7.** 22, 34 **8.** 37, 43
9. 12, 20

Page 141, Logical Strategy

1. D3 or G6 **2.** X's; D3 or G6 **3.** C2 or G6

Page 142, Steps in Order

Answers may vary. Suggestions follow, but accept all
correct student answers.
1. I, J, E, A, B, F, H, D, G, C, K
2. E, J, B, G, A, C, D, K, F, I, H

Page 143, Addition and Subtraction Logic

W + X = YZ
1. 1; $9 + 8$ is the highest combination possible.
2. 7; YZ is two digits, and Y can't be 0. **3.** 15;
Y has to be 1, so YZ is 15. **4.** 8; YZ is 15, and
$15 - 7 = 8$. **5.** 9 and 8; YZ is 17. The sum of W and
X must be 17.
AB − C = C
1. AB **2.** 1; The highest number C may is is 9, so
A has to be 1. **3.** even; An even number plus an
even number makes an even number, and an odd
number plus an odd number also makes an even
number. **4.** 2

Page 144, Sorting Numbers

1. 23, 29, 31; prime numbers **2.** 36, 49, 64, 81;
numbers squared **3.** 35, 40, 50; multiples of 5

4. 66, 77, 88; multiples of 11 **5.** 6, 21, 28;
triangular numbers **6.** 62, 71, 80; beginning with
17, add 9

Page 145, Deductive Logic

	Red	Green	Blue	White	Yellow
Akiko	X	X	X	X	O
Betty	X	X	O	X	X
Clara	X	X	X	O	X
Dana	O	X	X	X	X
Eve	X	O	X	X	X

Page 146, Sets and Circles

2.

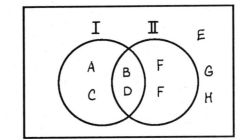

3.

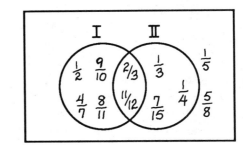

4.

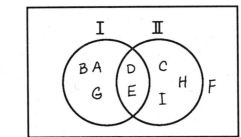

5.

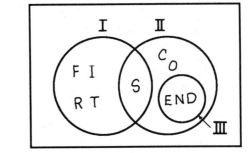

Page 147, Shape Families
1. A, C, F **2.** A Plig must have straight sides.
3. B, C, E **4.** A Klopper must have the same shape inside as outside.

Page 148, Number Logic
1. true **2.** true **3.** false **4.** false **5.** false
6. false **7.** false **8.** false **9.** false
10. false

Page 149, Make a Change
Answers may vary. Suggestions follow, but accept all correct student answers.
1. A prime number has exactly **two** distinct factors.
2. The sum of two odd numbers is an **even** number.
3. The **smallest** odd number that can be formed using all five odd digits is 1 less than 13, 580.
4. A triangle has exactly **three** sides. **5.** The sum of 2 three-digit numbers can contain at most **four** digits. **6.** In a division exercise, the dividend is equal to the divisor times the quotient **plus** the remainder. **7.** There are exactly **five** prime numbers between 30 and 50. **8.** The product of 2 two-digit numbers must contain at least **three** digits.
9. To multiply two fractions, you **multiply** the numerators and multiply the denominators. **10.** The product of an odd number and an even number is an **odd** number. **11.** Twenty-five percent is the same as one-**fourth**. **12.** The product of 2 three-digit numbers must contain either **six** or five digits.
13. Using the fewest number of coins to make 74¢ requires **two** dimes. **14.** The square root of an eight-digit number is at most a **four**-digit number.
15. The area formula for a circle **does** use the irrational number π.

Page 150, Logical Shapes

1.

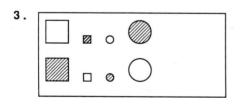

2.

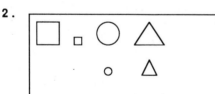

3.

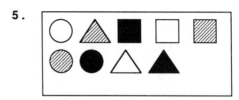

4.

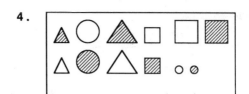

5.

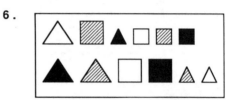

6.

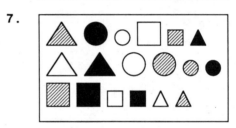

7.

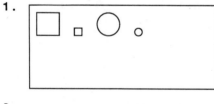

Page 151, Number Logic
1. $a = 5, b = 4$ **2.** $a = 5, b = 4$ **3.** $a = 6, b = 2$
4. $a = 7, b = 5$ **5.** $a = 5, b = 4$ **6.** $a = 7, b = 9$
7. $a = 0, b = 5$ **8.** $a = 5, b = 6$

Page 152, Mystery Words
1. NUMBER **2.** EQUAL **3.** AVERAGE
4. AREA **5.** LOGIC

Page 153, Number Juggling
In some cases, the order of these numbers may vary.
1. $12 \div 4 - 3 = 13$ **2.** $4 \times 3 - 12 = 0$
3. $12 - 4 - 3 = 5$ **4.** $4 \times 3 + 12 = 24$
5. $12 \div 3 + 4 = 8$ **6.** $12 \div 3 - 4 = 0$
7. $12 \div 4 \times 3 = 9$ **8.** $3 \times 4 + 12 = 1$
9. $12 \div 4 + 3 = 1$ **10.** $12 \times 3 \div 4 = 9$
11. $12 \times 3 - 4 = 32$

Page 154, Letter Logic
1. $2 \times 4 = 8; 4 \times 2 = 8$ **2.** $12 - 5 = 7$
3. $-11.$

A	B	C	D	E	F	G	H	I
4	8	2	7	6	1	9	5	3

  CRITICAL THINKING ACTIVITIES IN PATTERNS, IMAGERY, LOGIC Dale Seymour Publications

Page 155, Attributes
1. 1   2. 1   3. 4   4. 2   5. 2   6. 5   7. 8
8. 8   9. 7   10. 3   11. 3   12. 6

Page 156, Deductive Logic

	89	87	85	84	81
Maria	X	X	O	X	X
Tulsie	X	X	X	O	X
Ben	X	O	X	X	X
Harry	X	X	X	X	O
Kim	O	X	X	X	X

Page 157, Logical Conclusions
1. a. false   b. true   c. can't tell   d. can't tell
2. a. true   b. false   c. can't tell   d. true
e. true   f. can't tell   3. a. false   b. true
c. false   d. false   e. can't tell   f. false

Page 158, Deductive Reasoning
1. a. yes   b. no   c. yes   d. yes   e. no
2. a. no   b. yes   c. yes   d. yes   e. no
3. a. yes   b. yes   c. yes   d. no   e. no
f. yes   g. no   h. yes   i. yes   4. a. no
b. yes   c. yes   d. no   e. yes   f. no   g. yes
h. yes   i. yes